SIMPLIFY THE
Holidays

A **Reader's Digest Simpler Life**™ Book

Designed, edited, and produced by Weldon Owen

THE READER'S DIGEST ASSOCIATION, INC.

Group Editorial Director, Cooking/Home/Consumer Books Carol Guasti

Group Design Director, Cooking/Home/Consumer Books Joan Mazzeo

Project Editor Candace Conard

Project Art Director Jane Wilson

WELDON OWEN INC.

President John Owen

Publisher Roger S. Shaw

Series Editor Janet Goldenberg

Contributing Editors Mandy Erickson, Marianne Lipanovich

Copy Editors Lisa R. Bornstein, Gail Nelson

Art Director Elizabeth Marken

Design Consultant Emma Forge

Production Designer Brynn Breuner

Design Assistant William Erik Evans

Icon Illustrator Matt Graif

Production Director Stephanie Sherman

Production Manager Jen Dalton

Project Photographers Chris Shorten, Brian Pierce

Photo Stylist JoAnn Masaoka Van Atta

Photo Editor Melinda Lawson

A Reader's Digest/Weldon Owen Publication

Copyright © 1998 The Reader's Digest Association, Inc., and Weldon Owen Inc.

Library of Congress Cataloging in Publication Data has been applied for.

Printed in China

A note on weights and measures: Metric equivalences given for
U.S. weights and measures are approximate. Actual equivalences may vary.

SIMPLIFY THE
Holidays

ALLANA BARONI
WITH VICKI WEBSTER

Illustrations by JOHN HOLM

 Reader's Digest

The Reader's Digest Association, Inc.
Pleasantville, New York/Montreal

CONTENTS

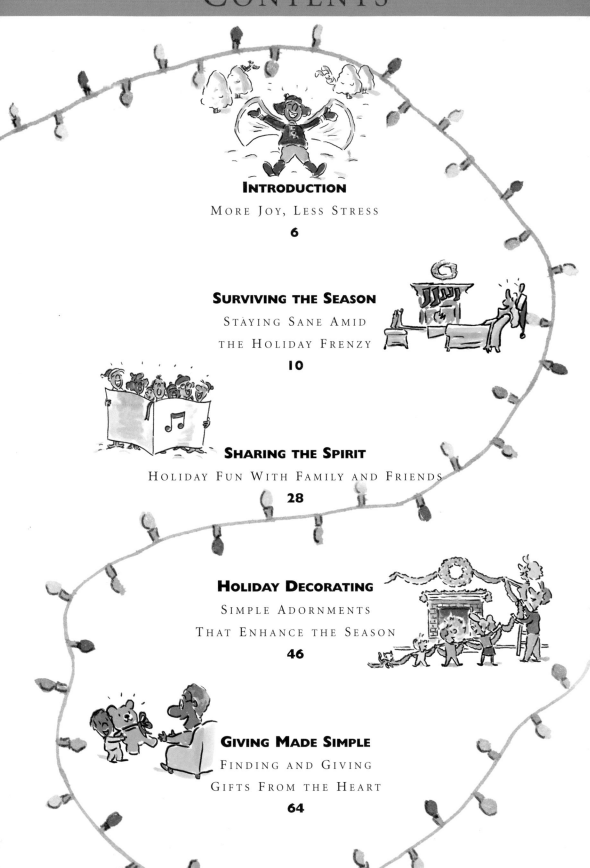

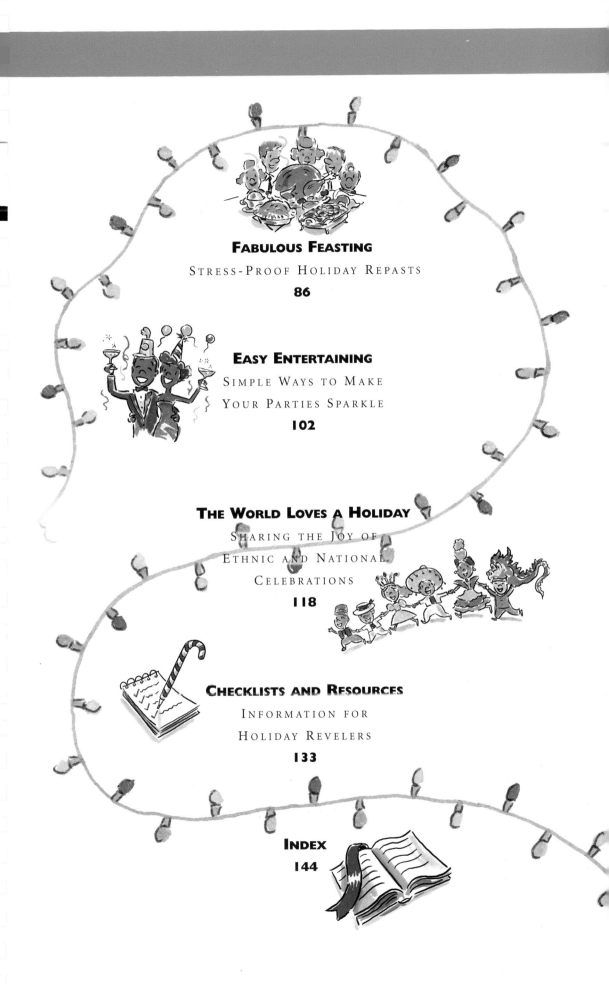

Simplifying your celebrations can
help make them more enjoyable.

MORE JOY, LESS STRESS

* ———— * ———— *

Who doesn't love a holiday? After all, what could be better than a day free of workaday cares—and filled with comforting surroundings, bountiful food and drink, and the fellowship of family and friends?

Unfortunately, however, the events leading up to this day of relaxation are often far from relaxing. Especially during the fall and winter, when holidays follow one another in quick succession, the demands of cooking, decorating, gift shopping, parties, and travel—on top of an already full schedule of work and household chores—can make the holiday whirl feel like a merry-go-round that's spinning out of control. Social pressures can add even more anxiety at holiday time, especially when family members come from differing ethnic or religious backgrounds, or when they must deal with the complexities of divorce and remarriage.

If you've ever felt overwhelmed by it all—if you've ever thought there *must* be a better way—here's some good news: There is. During my career as an event planner and gift consultant, I've developed a simple, foolproof approach to planning celebrations—be they Thanksgiving feasts, Christmas open houses, Hanukkah parties, or Fourth of July barbecues. I've learned how to concentrate on producing fun and good times while eliminating extra work and anxiety.

With the help of Vicki Webster, I'll share my organizational secrets with you. You'll learn how to manage every aspect of your seasonal celebrations, from planning festive adventures to orchestrating big family feasts. You'll learn how to decorate simply and quickly to achieve dazzling effects without using up precious free time. In these pages you'll also find a host of shopping tips, from simple gift ideas to hints on one-stop sources of presents to please everyone on your list. You'll discover how you can entertain your family, your friends, and your coworkers graciously and easily, so that you can enjoy the gatherings as much as they do.

You'll find a whole chapter filled with traditions from many cultures that you can borrow to make your own celebrations richer. And at the end of the book there's a selection of checklists and resources to help keep you organized and inspired. In short, *Simplify the Holidays* gives you all the raw material you need to take the stress out of your holiday celebrations and put the meaning—and the fun—back in.

Ilana Ba

Take time to enjoy the simple pleasures of the season.

Simple Symbols

———— ✳ ————

IN EACH CHAPTER OF THIS BOOK you'll find nuggets of advice for simplifying every aspect of the holidays—from planning a Thanksgiving feast for the extended family to finding gifts for older relatives who claim they don't need anything. These quick tips will help you relax and enjoy the holidays despite all your obligations. Look for boxes marked with symbols in the following categories.

 Labor Savers help you ease your holiday chores whenever it seems there's just too much you need to do. Refer to these boxes to find out how to get more done with less effort so you'll be able to kick back and enjoy the festivities.

 Time Savers explain how to shave minutes or even hours from shopping, cooking, and other holiday tasks—without compromising your celebration plans. Follow these tips so you can spend more time visiting with friends and relatives.

 Bright Ideas offer tips for buying gifts, planning celebrations, managing family conflict, and keeping the little ones occupied throughout the holiday festivities. These ideas—like many important concepts—are surprisingly easy to implement.

 Simply Safer suggestions offer ways to reduce your risks over the holidays. They provide tips for safe decorating and celebrating, including one on how to prevent guests from overimbibing. Just one of these simple tips could avoid a rush to the hospital—at least they'll make your celebrations worry free.

 Stress Busters provide simple, surefire methods to avoid family conflict and to resist being overwhelmed by the pressures of the holidays. These tips will help you relieve holiday stress so you can enjoy each day's festivities with peace of mind.

 Cost Cutters show you how to make the most of your holiday budget by shopping and spending wisely. Whether you are buying in bulk for a holiday feast or searching for the perfect gift, these suggestions can help you keep expenses low.

 Rules of Thumb give you some guidelines in planning how much wine, beer, liquor, and other bar supplies you'll need for holiday parties; best times to avoid the crowds while shopping for gifts; and strategies for overcoming those holiday blues.

 Don't Forget tips offer ideas to remember that may seem obvious at first but are easy to forget during the hustle and bustle of tasks you must attend to at holiday time. These boxes provide handy reminders for everything from easing your workload to increasing the fun for everyone during the holiday season.

TOWARD a carefree
Celebration

— ✳ —

1 Identify the aspects of the holidays that are most important to you—family **togetherness,** the spirit of the season, religious traditions—and focus your energies on those areas. **2** Counter the pressure to consume by focusing on family **activities** rather than exchanging gifts. **3** Decide as a **family** which holidays you want to focus on, and how, where, and with whom you want to celebrate. **4** If you and your spouse are of different **faiths,** enrich the season by honoring both traditions. **5** When you find yourself alone over the holidays, **treat** yourself to a favorite meal, a good book—even a vacation. **6** Book **help**—caterers, babysitters, travel agents—as far in advance as possible. **7** Decide which responsibilities you want to **delegate** to family members or friends. **8** **Shop early** for presents, decorations, nonperishable foods, and party supplies. **9** Make time for exercise and the occasional **indulgence**—and don't feel guilty. **10** Record what goes well and what doesn't for a winning **strategy** next year. ●

SURVIVING
THE SEASON

STAYING SANE AMID THE HOLIDAY FRENZY

* —— * —— *

There's no doubt about it: All holidays can be stressful. But the period between October and January, when major celebrations come one right after the other, can take anxiety over the top. Chances are the real culprit is not the crowd at the shopping mall, the price tag on the computer your son wants, or the fact that Aunt Evelyn won't come to Christmas dinner if Uncle George is going to be there. More likely, it's an unrealistic notion about what the holidays should be.

The solution? Banish that idea of the "perfect holiday" from your head. Admitting that you can't stage a chain of flawless holiday celebrations—and that you really aren't even inclined to try—doesn't make you Ebenezer Scrooge. On the contrary, focusing on traditions that have real meaning for you and your loved ones—and making plans to cope with the expectations of the season—will make all the holidays more relaxing for everyone in your family.

IT'S YOUR CELEBRATION

---✳---

I F THE APPEARANCE OF THE FIRST FALL PUMPKINS MAKES YOU NERVOUS ABOUT HOW YOU'LL GET THROUGH THE NEXT SEVERAL MONTHS OF TURKEYS, TREES, PARTIES, PRESENTS, AND VISITING RELATIVES, YOU'RE IN GOOD COMPANY.

Blame it on modern times, but the season of joy can sometimes seem more like a season of stress—a time of crowded stores and roadways, high prices, and magnified family differences. Add the pressures of year-end work schedules, kids wishing for all the hot new toys they see on television, and flu viruses waiting to attack at every turn, and it's a wonder that anyone can muddle through at all—much less tackle those projects without which (many of us are led to believe) no holiday would be complete, such as creating a scale model of Windsor Castle out of gingerbread.

The good news is that you can send the Grinch packing if you want to. Start by identifying the stress points that keep you from enjoying the holiday season to the fullest. Then look for creative ways to relieve the stress. And don't worry if your initial efforts fall short of the mark—just chalk them up to experience and take a different approach the next time.

HOLIDAY BUGABOOS

The first step toward enjoying, rather than merely enduring, this time of the year is to identify what bothers you most about the holidays and to see if there's a way you can alter the scene—even if it's nothing more

Shopping for gifts *can be the biggest holiday stressor. Reduce the pressure by giving fewer presents or taking a family trip instead.*

than a change in attitude. People prone to holiday funk point to all manner of seasonal irritations, but they pretty much fall into a few broad categories:

Pressure to consume. Many people claim this is their biggest source of annoyance at Christmas or Hanukkah, and it *is* easy to feel backed into a corner, especially if you have small children. It's only natural that you want your kids to laugh with delight when they open their holiday gifts. But it's tempting to go overboard, especially when both parents work: Mom and Dad often try to make up for time spent at the office by lavishing gifts on their children.

There's also pressure to consume piles of sweet, rich food during the holiday season. It's hard to say no when your father will be devastated if you don't take a slice of his famous pecan pie, or your neighbor's kids proudly present you with a box of sugar cookies coated in frosting.

Perfectionism. Many people like to make their surroundings visually appealing, but some embark on an all-out quest

Familiar Faces

Part of the stress of the holidays for children—especially if your relatives live far away—is being greeted by a houseful of "strangers" at family gatherings. Before you go over the river to Grandma's house, sit down with your kids and the photo albums. Tell family stories to remind them who their relatives are and why you'll be visiting them.

step, how to make everything from a stenciled tablecloth to quilted place mats and wreaths made of dried flowers.

Family strife. Fifties sitcoms notwithstanding, every family has its differences, ranging from minor personality conflicts to raging feuds. At most times of the year family members who are not particularly close don't socialize, and the differences are

The first step toward combating holiday stress is to identify what bothers you most—and to see if there's a way to change things.

for perfection. Perhaps they grew up with parents and other relatives who executed elaborate seasonal celebrations. Or they mistake the spreads in glossy lifestyle magazines for realistic portrayals of people's lives, rather than what they are—the collaborative effort of droves of editors, art directors, decorators, chefs, and photo stylists. Or they've seen too many TV shows in which the host demonstrates, step by

ignored. Come the holidays, though, the scene changes. Relatives who rarely choose to see each other are suddenly thrown into each other's company for hours, even days. Add to this involuntary togetherness everyone's normal load of holiday pressure; toss in some common winter ingredients such as icy roads, delayed flight schedules, and bad head colds; spice things up with differences in politics, religion, income, or social standing; douse it all with alcohol and overeating, and voilà! You've got a recipe for instant discord.

Lonesome-ranger letdown. Even people who are solitary by nature often prefer to celebrate special times with others, and some people find the thought of being alone on any holiday—especially Thanksgiving, Christmas, or New Year's—particularly difficult. The fact is, even the most gregarious reveler winds up flying solo now and then. Even if the cause is something as unavoidable as a canceled flight that leaves you stranded 2,000 miles from home, involuntary solitude can put a damper on the best of spirits.

No-name blues. Many people say they don't know why the holidays get them down. The cause might be some or all of the stresses already mentioned, rolled into one giant funk. It might be unpleasant memories too deeply buried to surface,

Holiday Wishes

Guide young children away from materialism by making family wishes for the holiday season. On Christmas Eve or the first night of Hanukkah, gather the family together. Instead of talking about what gifts kids will receive, have everyone make a wish, such as that Cousin Susie will get the job she wants or that a neighbor will get well.

or the result of a lifelong habit of gazing at the cloud instead of the silver lining. It could even be a response to the short days and long nights of early winter.

CHANGES IN ATTITUDE

Need help in fighting your own personal Grinch? Start by realizing that you're not a pawn in the hands of aggressive advertisers, harried fellow shoppers, and bickering relatives. Some annoying situations you can change, others you can just walk away from—and you can always adjust your attitude. Uncle Willard gets tipsy at every holiday gathering and tries to dance up the wall like Fred Astaire? Think of it as fodder for an amusing family anecdote and assign ol' twinkle toes a designated driver. Everyone else at the office goes skiing and leaves all the work to you? What a great chance to get things done and make your star shine! Your ex-spouse flies off to the Bahamas with the kids? Now's your chance to sleep in every morning and go out to dinner every night, cruise the art galleries at your leisure, or even escape to a sun-baked isle of your own.

Don't get the wrong idea—no one's suggesting that you try out for sainthood or that you hide from all the "real-life" issues. But some psychological studies have shown that life does flow more smoothly for those people who see the cup as half full rather than half empty.

SCALING BACK

Whether your reaction to seasonal sales pressure stems from financial constraints or simply from the conviction that the

The best holidays are those spent treasuring one another's company.

overload express has gone far enough, you don't have to play the more-is-better game. Granted, marching to your own drummer is easier in a grown-ups-only parade; with

Instead of spending money on a pile of gifts, take the family on a holiday trip. You'll shift the emphasis from consumerism to togetherness.

kids on the scene, the situation is more complex. But you can still trim the holiday excess with minimal trauma. With toddlers and young children, it's a cinch—they're delighted with whatever glittering treasures Santa leaves under the tree. With older kids and adults, you can address the issue directly. Simply say that you feel the gift giving has gotten out of hand and that you would like to cut back this year. You might even be surprised by their positive

reaction: Maybe everyone else felt the same way but no one one wanted to be the first person to say it.

If you encounter any objections, stick to your guns. You can lessen the shock by cutting back a little every year; deflect attention from the holiday "gimmes" by focusing on family activities or charity rather than gift exchanges.

If you're convinced that you simply can't survive another year with a mound of presents resembling Mount McKinley, go cold turkey: Take everyone away on a holiday trip. You might spend about as much money as you would have on gifts, but you'll still have shifted the emphasis from consumerism to family togetherness.

THE PERFECTION BUG

If your neighbor drives you batty with the perfect wreaths hanging in every window of his immaculate home, if the televised

If holiday decorating *sets your heart aglow, go all out—but cut back on other time-consuming activities such as cooking.*

image of a woman making crazy-quilt tea cozies from her kids' outgrown flannel pajamas sets your teeth on edge, here's a solution: Ignore it all and go your own way. Send store-bought cards. Deck the front door with the pinecone wreath that you've had for 20 years. Buy cookies at the bakery instead of making your own. Don't worry about what the lights on the house next door to yours looks like, and don't watch those how-to-make-the-holidays-perfect television shows. Discover the liberating power of the Off button.

STRIKING A BALANCE

On the other hand, maybe you love everything about the season, and have since childhood: the sparkling lights and the warm glow of candles, the glorious music and magical aromas, the festive parties and homes decked out in their holiday

best, even the bustle of shopping. You plunge in with a vengeance when you feel the first nip in the air. That's great, as long as you enjoy all the hoopla and don't wake up every New Year's morning exhausted, swearing you'll never do it again.

The trick is to strike a balance between making so much fuss that you feel drained of energy, goodwill, and cash, and making so little effort that the holidays don't feel special. You can produce a memorable celebration and maintain your sanity even without an army of chefs and decorators at your disposal. Just set your sights a shade this side of perfection. Choose the one or two traditions you care about most—the open house you've always had on Christmas Eve, for instance, or the weekend you spend baking dozens of cookies you send to friends and family scattered around the world. Focus your time and energy on the projects you enjoy most, and cut back on others. Forget making needlepoint tree ornaments for all your cousins; buy some nice blown-glass ones instead. Give up your annual trek to the tree farm to harvest the perfect Douglas fir; take everyone to the corner lot or pick up the telephone and have one delivered.

If you can't bear to do that—if you love it all too much to give up anything for good—try rotating the emphasis: Each year, choose one holiday for which you pull out all the stops, and let the rest remain low key. For example, your black-tie New Year's Eve gala might take center stage one year. The next year you confine this celebration to a quiet evening by the fire with smoked salmon and champagne for two—or attend someone else's party—and the holiday star is Thanksgiving dinner for both sides of your extended family and the friends, neighbors, and coworkers whose company you enjoy most.

FAMILY DISCORD

Family differences can take on almost as many forms and degrees of intensity as there are families, but setting a few basic rules can ease the tension all around.

Christmas tree *and* a Hanukkah menorah, a Passover seder *and* an Easter-egg hunt. Look at the traditions of your spouse's family not as challenges to your own religious heritage but as fertile ground for adding more meaning—and fun—to the holidays that your family celebrates.

As for the trials and tribulations of family get-togethers, it's a matter of degree. If differences between family members are too intense to face, don't force it, especially

If you and your spouse come from different backgrounds, look at each other's traditions as ways to add more meaning to the holidays.

In situations where in-laws compete for attention—an almost universal occurrence in new marriages—be democratic. If geography allows, divide your visiting time equally; if not, alternate homes each year, even if you clearly prefer one side. If the major sticking points stem from divorce—rancorous or otherwise—make one unbreakable vow: The kids come first. If you and your spouse come from different religious backgrounds, the holidays can be a lens for magnifying differences, especially if you have children. The rituals associated with Christmas or Easter, Hanukkah or Passover, may be joyful reminders for one parent but added stresses for the other. If one of you takes your faith more seriously than the other or if the trappings of one holiday are more appealing, children may be swayed toward one religion, and silent resentment may build between you.

Rather than feel threatened by your partner's traditions, view diversity as an opportunity to enrich the season. Have a

if you're convinced that a heart-to-heart ahead of time will have no effect. Instead, spend the holidays at home with your immediate family, or go on a trip.

But maybe what rankles you the most is simply the fact that all you really have in common with some of your relatives is

Neutral Territory

If differences in wealth, social standing, religion, or ethnic background make it hard for some family members to spend time together, try holding your holiday gathering in a neutral setting. Everyone is likely to feel more at ease in a rented house, a resort, or even a restaurant, where personal issues will take a backseat to the setting.

a few strands of DNA. Try this experiment one year. Pretend you're a humorist such as James Thurber or a novelist like Anne Tyler. Then just sit back, watch, and listen. Remind yourself that for an observer of humanity there's no such thing as a bad experience—it's all material.

ON YOUR OWN

Even if you can't be with your loved ones on holidays—or if you've decided it's not worth the stress—you don't have to go it alone. Rally the other stay-behinds in your apartment building and throw yourselves an "Orphans' Thanksgiving." Call a children's hospital, nursing home, local soup kitchen, or hospice and volunteer for the day. Take a cruise, book yourself into a resort, or take a tour to a place you've always wanted to see. Don't limit yourself to singles venues; rather, choose destinations or activities that appeal to you for their own sake—a theater-and-shopping trip in London, perhaps, or a resort with a world-class golf course. (It's more fun to meet people with whom you have more in common than mere singlehood.)

If all else fails, be shameless: Call a friend whose family you like and casually let it be known that you'll be alone for the holiday. You're almost guaranteed to get

> **Call a friend and casually let it be known that you'll be alone for the holidays. You're almost sure to get a dinner invitation.**

an invitation to dinner. If you don't, try another friend. Keep trying. And if a misunderstanding with a family member or close friend is keeping you from sharing the holiday, maybe the season of goodwill is the time to bury the hatchet.

The holidays can be relaxing even
if your plans go awry.

What if you've made your visiting plans, however, and an unpredicted blizzard on Christmas Eve leaves you stranded in your home? Or your intended hostess calls on Thanksgiving morning and announces that her furnace has broken and she'll be taking refuge elsewhere? Or an emergency work deadline forces you to cancel a New Year's visit with friends in a distant city? You could choose to be lonely and miserable, or you could enjoy this chance to indulge yourself. Cook your favorite dinner or take yourself to a restaurant that's open on the holiday. Light a fire and curl up with a book. Put on some soothing music and soak in a hot bubble bath. Make a big bowl of popcorn and watch a favorite video. Or pick up that long-neglected sketchbook and head outside. You might discover that when you're alone you're in very good company.

THE NO-NAME BLUES

This is your holiday, and you don't have to be jolly if you don't want to. But the season of light will come and go whether you want it to or not. You say you've contemplated all the common sources of holiday annoyance, reasoned everything out to the best of your ability, and the festivities still get you down? Don't try to cure the disease, just treat the symptoms.

Start by writing your troubles down: Simply getting things off your chest can help you feel better. Next, get some books and tapes on combating negativity, and do the exercises they recommend. Steer clear of the ones that urge you to affirm in buoyant tones that you are prosperous,

Do Unto Others

Nothing will lift your spirits as much as helping someone who needs and appreciates it. If you are feeling blue, volunteer for a church group or homeless shelter, help out at a gift drive for poor children and their families, or visit a retirement center— there are plenty of people with no family nearby who would love to have some holiday company.

healthy, and surrounded by loved ones. Look instead for titles that acknowledge life's negatives but focus on the positives (see page 142 for one suggestion).

The best way by far to beat the no-name blues—and all the other stresses of the holiday season—is to cultivate your sense of humor. Spend some time every day enjoying whatever tickles your funny bone—*The Far Side* cartoons, P. G. Wodehouse stories, reruns of *The Mary Tyler Moore Show,* that old copy of *One Hundred and One Elephant Jokes* stashed on the top shelf of your bookcase.

You can also find humor in the holidays themselves. You may not find every event amusing—say, your cat leaping onto the Christmas tree, sending it crashing down on the robot you just spent all night putting together. But if you do enough chuckling and guffawing, you'll find that the world does indeed start to look different, and maybe not so bad after all.

A WINNING STRATEGY

---*---

NOW THAT YOU'VE CONTEMPLATED THE BIG PICTURE, IT'S TIME TO BUCKLE DOWN AND MAP OUT A GAME PLAN THAT WILL HELP YOU AVOID MANY OF THE SEASON'S FRUSTRATIONS AND MAKE TIME FOR MEANINGFUL CELEBRATION.

The first step is a simple matter of viewpoint. Instead of seeing the fall and winter holidays as isolated dates—Halloween followed by a lull, then Thanksgiving, a second lull, then the ready-or-not arrival of Christmas or Hanukkah and New Year's—visualize them as one unit. Sit down with everyone in your family who's old enough to realize that you can't do it all alone and plan your strategy. Choose which celebrations you'll pull out all the stops for and which ones you'll keep low key—or consign to others for host duty.

Not that good planning will solve all your holiday woes—no matter how well organized you are, the season can still bring a few surprises. You could be felled by a bad head cold the morning of your New Year's Eve party. Your car could break down on the way to your spouse's parents' house for Thanksgiving—and you're the one bringing the turkey. And, yes, you may end up dashing to the convenience store at 10 P.M. Christmas Eve for a quart of milk and a roll of toilet paper. However, the more you do to head off uncertainty,

You'll have an easier jog through the holidays
if you plan your route in advance.

and the sooner in the year you do it, the easier it will be for you to relax and enjoy every part of the holiday season.

SCHEDULING

To get the ball rolling, buy a calendar with plenty of space for writing. Mark all the standard holidays your family celebrates between mid-October and the end of the year, such as Halloween, Thanksgiving, Christmas, Hanukkah, Kwanzaa, and New Year's Eve. Then add any occasions already scheduled that demand your time over the winter: that out-of-town conference, your sister's wedding, your company's board of directors meeting or office party, your father's birthday.

If the calendar already has more filled-in squares than blank ones, resolve to add a gentle but firm "no, thank you" to your vocabulary and use it whenever you feel the pressure starting to build.

Next, call a family conference and decide how, when, where, and with whom you want to spend each upcoming holiday.

Kid Power

Include children in holiday chores as much as possible. They can update your card list on a computer, print it onto mailing labels, then stick the labels onto envelopes. Younger helpers are also dandy at affixing stamps and labels once you show them the ropes. The kids will have fun and help ease your burden at the same time.

account. Maybe you and your spouse are both juggling the responsibilities of high-pressure jobs and graduate school, and all either of you wants from Santa is a good, long nap and a few more days in the week. Or maybe for months you've thought of little else but watching your 14-month-old daughter toddle toward the tree on Christmas morning in the company of

Plan the holiday that will be the happiest and most meaningful for your family—not the one others think you should have.

Really listen to what the kids have to say; their priorities may well surprise you— they may be tired of *The Nutcracker,* even though you scrimped and saved for tickets every year because you thought it was the highlight of their season. Discuss the circumstances of your lives at the moment. Maybe you've just bought a new house or sent the twins off to college, and you're feeling a distinct pinch in your bank

her cousins and doting grandparents, and you'd be terribly blue if you didn't splurge on tickets to go back home.

Remember, this is not a quiz. There are no right or wrong answers. Plan whatever will make the happiest, most meaningful holiday for you and your family— not the one your grandmother had or the one the editors of your favorite magazine are promoting this year. Above all, be

Build in time *for laughter and togetherness as well as for getting things done. Even a busy schedule can make room for both.*

realistic about how much you can — or want to—accomplish, and how much celebrating you can comfortably afford.

Next, take a good look at each holiday you've put on your schedule and what it entails. If you know when the holiday celebrations are taking place, jot down the dates; if not, rough approximations will work just fine. Ask yourself some pertinent questions: What plans do you have for entertaining this season—a big open house, a few dinner parties for friends, a family gathering for Thanksgiving? When, and for how long, will you have overnight guests? Will you need the services of caterers, housecleaners, florists, or babysitters?

Notice how often activities repeat— how many times your plans call for entertaining overnight guests; cooking for a crowd; or sending out mailings, whether in the form of party invitations, Christmas cards, or thank-you notes. That analysis gets you to the next step: Buy a notebook small enough to tuck into your pocket or handbag, and start jotting down all the things you'll need to buy over the entire holiday period—from wrapping paper and ribbon to candles, mailing labels, tape, and extra chairs for the dining room.

TAKING INVENTORY

Move another step toward a trouble-free holiday season by taking a household inventory. Is your guest room ready for visitors? If the sheets are wearing thin or the clock battery has died, replace them now, before your boss and her husband drop in for coffee after the office party and end up spending the night because of a sudden ice storm. Check your closets for any items in poor repair or short supply, and list these in your notebook. If the kids have outgrown their boots or your favorite gloves are missing, now is the time to find out—not the night before you're set to leave on a ski trip.

HOLIDAY TIMETABLE

✳

THE BIG FALL AND WINTER HOLIDAYS—Halloween, Thanksgiving, Christmas, Hanukkah, Kwanzaa, and New Year's—arrive in quick succession. By planning for them over the course of the year and by consolidating tasks whenever you can, you'll feel more relaxed when they roll around. Here's a timetable to help you plan.

	January–September	October	November	December
PLANNING				
Update holiday card list and addresses	●			
Browse magazines; create master file of holiday ideas		●		
Coordinate holiday plans with family		●		
Make holiday travel reservations		●		
Plan holiday parties		●	●	
Finalize holiday menus			●	●
SHOPPING AND COOKING				
Comb stores and mail-order catalogs for gifts	●	●	●	●
Pick up party goods at discount supply houses	●	●	●	●
Purchase bulk Halloween candy at warehouse outlets		●		
Make and freeze holiday baked goods		●	●	
Buy nonperishable food and drink for holiday gatherings		●	●	
Buy frozen turkeys for Thanksgiving and Christmas			●	
Buy perishables and prepared dishes			●	●
Pick up last-minute gifts				●
Hit after-holiday sales for cards, decorations, wrapping paper				●
SHIPPING AND MAILING				
Mail holiday party invitations			●	●
Send presents to out-of-town family and friends				●
Mail holiday cards				●
DECORATING				
Sort and discard decorations you no longer use	●	●	●	●
Gather and store decorations good for any holiday	●	●	●	●
Make or purchase Halloween costumes		●		
Pick out Christmas tree and wreaths				●
Buy Hanukkah or Kwanzaa candles				●
Set up decorations and wrap last-minute items				●

PUTTING YOUR PLAN INTO MOTION

---✳---

ONCE YOU'VE DECIDED WHERE YOU WANT TO FOCUS YOUR ENERGY OVER THE HOLIDAY SEASON, YOU CAN SPRING INTO ACTION. FIRST, FREE UP TIME FOR FESTIVE ENDEAVORS BY GETTING MUNDANE DETAILS OUT OF THE WAY.

Calendar in hand, pick up the phone and make calls to the vet, the hairdresser, the dentist, the pediatrician, the housecleaner, the car mechanic—anyone whose routine services you or your family will need over the course of the holiday season.

Then move on to special events. If you know in October that your family will be going away from Christmas Eve through New Year's weekend, call your travel agent and book everything you'll need—plane, hotel, and restaurant reservations; theater tickets and rental cars.

Ask for Help

Many people assume their loved ones will automatically know that they need help with chores, and then become upset when no one pitches in. When you need help preparing for the holidays, ask (pleasantly and early) before you find yourself doing all the cooking, shopping, and decorating. Family members will probably be glad to help out.

Arrange for a pet sitter and for someone to water your plants, pick up the mail, and check the house from time to time. If you need a caterer and a florist for your big Hanukkah party—even if you aren't ready to discuss details—call both and ask if they can reserve the date. You will stand a better chance of booking the dates you need. You'll also win the gratitude of those professionals who spend too much of every holiday season fielding last-minute—and often unrealistic—requests.

SAVING YOUR SANITY

It's an annoying fact of life that, no matter how much you might want to give yourself over to holiday festivities, the real world carries on as usual. Kids still have to be fed, bathed, and driven to school. Cars, clothes, and dogs still get dirty and have to be washed. Your boss still expects you to show up for work. Fortunately, there are time-honored ways of coping. Here are some of the best:

Forget perfection. That goes for your housekeeping as well as your decor. It's unlikely that the morning newscast will show up to film your Kwanzaa celebration—and if it does, it's not going to be videotaping the dust behind the sofa.

Delegate. Turn over full responsibility for some everyday chores or holiday tasks— or both—to other family members. True, you will have to relinquish control: Your 12-year-old may not load the dishwasher as neatly as you do, and the star your spouse buys for the Christmas tree might not be the one you'd choose. But you'll still have gained much by freeing up time for yourself and giving family members a sense of inclusion in holiday preparations. (You might even discover that your daughter has a hidden talent for making hand-painted wrapping paper or that your son is a budding short-order cook.)

Buy time. Hire a housecleaning service for a day or once a week during the holiday season. It could be just the relief you need to get the house ready for entertaining or to clean up afterward. Pay a neighborhood teen to watch the kids, do the shopping, wash the car, or take the dog for a walk.

Delegate responsibility to other family members. You'll relinquish some control, but you'll also free up valuable time for yourself.

Put it off. During the holiday season cut out appointments that clutter the calendar. Skip your book group for December. Cancel this month's bridge club session. Play hooky from the dog's obedience school. (One caveat: Do not give up anything that truly rejuvenates you or helps maintain your sanity—whether it's your daily jog, a weekly yoga class, or the monthly lecture series at the art museum.)

Picking out a Christmas tree *is a holiday "chore" that the whole family can do together. Take the time to turn it into a fun excursion.*

Combine your efforts. Practice the useful art of doing two things at once. Read catalogs while you ride the bike at the gym. Take your Christmas cards to the dentist's office and address them while you wait. When you're baking Halloween cookies, make an extra batch in Christmas shapes and stash them in the freezer; if you're baking pies for Thanksgiving, make and freeze extras for Christmas. When you call your spa to book a massage, order a gift certificate for a friend—or for everybody on your list. (Boy, will you be popular.)

SHOPPING EARLY

Without question, the greatest gobbler of time at the holidays—and for most people the greatest source of stress—is shopping. It doesn't matter whether you're out for gifts, party supplies, or a jar of peanut

It's never too early in the year to shop for gifts and holiday supplies.

butter—you can bet your last coupon that from the day after Thanksgiving until just before Christmas the lines will be long, the parking lots full, and the clerks harassed and surly. But there are some easy ways you can avoid the madness.

The first technique is to recognize that it's never too early to buy supplies. Begin with trips to local discount warehouses—

Before you've planned a single menu, you can stock up on staples with a long shelf life. Look for sales on favorite items.

those gargantuan places that sell everything from tomato sauce to computer paper in huge quantities at bargain prices.

Travel with your pocket notebook, a playful spirit, and an open mind (though not necessarily an open wallet). Think how a certain item could serve you many different ways. A few hundred yards of red ribbon, for instance, will not only get you

through Christmas, Valentine's Day, and the Fourth of July; it will also look festive teamed up with bright yellow paper on a birthday present. A crate of white candles will furnish enough glow power to endure through all your holiday parties plus a season's worth of power outages.

Now think about food. Before you've planned a single menu, you can stock up on staples with a long shelf life. Watch for bargains on good brands of chicken broth, olives, canned tomatoes—anything you need for favorite recipes. (Resist the temptation of a great price on an unknown label—inferior quality is never a bargain.) Look for sales on your favorite wines, spirits, and mixers, and buy enough to last through a season or more of parties, dinners, and special holiday toasts.

TAKING STOCK

As the season progresses, take careful notes on what works and what doesn't. Don't forget to keep track of all your holiday-related expenses. You might even want to make sketches or take snapshots of your successful efforts—anything that may be helpful the next time around. Keep everything in a three-ring binder. Jot down information about the babysitter the kids adored, the travel agent who found your family a bargain flight at the last minute, or the yoga class that got you through the season with your good humor intact.

If everyone at your party raved about the Viennese torte you served on New Year's Eve, note what cookbook it came from or what bakery you bought it from. Conversely, if it bombed, note that in your planner and in the cookbook itself. If you shopped for everything from smoked salmon to cocktail napkins in one mail-order catalog, put it in the book. Take particular note of when things went on sale; stores tend to repeat successful sale patterns year after year.

After you've swept up the last fleck of New Year's confetti, sent out your final thank-you note, and had time to reflect on the festivities of the past few months, ask yourself whether a unified approach to the holiday season worked for you. Did plotting out your game plan early help you and your family to relax, enjoy yourselves, and focus your attention on the true meaning of the holidays? Were you able to maintain your effort throughout the season?

If the answers are yes, carry on for next year: When February arrives and the sap starts rising in the trees, gather the family around the table, get out your binder full of tips and resources, and start formulating your holiday game plan for the upcoming year. A whole season of festivities lies ahead, stretching from Valentine's Day to Labor Day, and the choices for celebrating (or not) are yours to make.

STRESS-FREE ways to
Share THE Days

—✳—

1 Separate the holiday **traditions** that bring you joy from the ones that don't work for you anymore (or never did). **2** Involve the whole family in the **planning** process and be willing to compromise. **3** Schedule one or two extra-special activities that the family can enjoy together during the holidays, such as a nature walk or an evening at the skating rink. **4** Use the holidays as springboards for **teaching** kids about history, other cultures, and the true spirit of the season. **5** Make **giving** to the less fortunate a part of your holiday tradition. Have your kids donate old toys or participate in a food drive to teach them about charity. **6** Make time for **romance.** **7** Use your imagination and a little advance planning to put your holiday **houseguests** at ease—or to be the perfect houseguest yourself. **8** Let family members and guests **pitch in** with the holiday chores whenever they're willing. **9** Send cards, videos, or e-mail to help you stay **in touch** with friends and family members you won't be able to see in person. ●

SHARING THE SPIRIT

HOLIDAY FUN WITH FAMILY AND FRIENDS

* —— ✳ —— *

Holidays are that rarity in the modern world: a sanctioned break from the demands of work and school—a time for parents and children to reconnect, a time to enjoy the company of relatives and friends. Making your way through the maze of holiday rituals can be tricky, however. The distance separating family members often means that a visit turns into a weeklong camp-out instead of an afternoon at Grandma's. Divorce, blended families, and a multicultural society call for new codes of etiquette and understanding.

But today's world brings conveniences as well as complexity—from the ease of catalog shopping to the instantaneous communication of the Internet. Assisted by those standbys of savvy revelers—flexibility, imagination, and planning—you can make any holiday special and keep the emphasis where it belongs: on family fun and togetherness.

Seasons of Joy

——— ✳ ———

MANY PEOPLE DREAD THE HOLIDAYS EACH YEAR BECAUSE THEY BRING YET ANOTHER ROUND OF TRADITIONS THAT HAVE GROWN TIRESOME. YET TRY AS THEY MIGHT, THEY CAN'T SEEM TO THINK OF A BETTER WAY.

If you think life is too short for rituals that make you feel harried rather than happy, or jealous rather than joyous, the question is simple: How do you change old routines without offending the people who are near and dear to you? The answer: gently but firmly—after all, it's not as if you don't still love your family. If the prospect of preparing for another Christmas gathering leaves you drained, if you're tired of deciding who will host Thanksgiving dinner or the annual Fourth of July barbecue and reunion, you can simply opt out. You don't have to offer detailed explanations. Just say you'd like to try something different this year—for example, you've decided to stay home with the kids, or to take them on a trip. If you still enjoy big gatherings but want to break with tradition, offer your extended family some alternatives—such as going out to a restaurant together. The rest of the clan might actually agree that a change is long overdue.

THE ART OF COMPROMISE

The same thing goes for rituals your immediate family follows every year. Do you deck the house each Christmas with so many lights that astronauts can see it from orbit—despite the fact that the routine results in bashed thumbs and sore tempers? Do you drive to the same park each year to watch the Fourth of July fireworks, even though the mosquitoes are terrible? It might be high time for your family to try a less stressful agenda.

You may well discover that you, your spouse, and your kids all have very different notions of holiday fun. Perhaps every year you look forward to watching the Macy's Thanksgiving Day Parade on TV with your kids, but your eldest gets bored with it. Maybe the sounds of a football game punctuating the haze of New Year's Day drive you up the wall, but your husband couldn't survive without his annual game-watching brunch.

Dueling Agendas

If both sets of grandparents want the kids at their gatherings, ask for proposed dates well in advance. Reconcile the schedules as soon as you can— you'll avoid disappointments and wounded feelings. This is especially important in blended families, when three or more sets of grandparents may be in contention for children's time.

The best solution may be to compromise. Spend an hour watching the parade with your youngest, then move to the kitchen and work on dinner with your eldest. Let your husband gather his football crowd in front of the set at your place on January 1 while you and some old friends convene elsewhere to watch the Vienna Philharmonic's New Year's Day concert on TV.

If holiday rituals make you feel harried rather than happy, tell your family gently but firmly that it's time to change the old routines.

Your sensitivity and tact may be tested if yours is a mixed-religion family. If you are Christian, you probably rejoice in having a Christmas tree with all the trimmings—yet you know that it alienates your Jewish spouse. What to do? Maybe you can keep the lavish tree, but also have a Hanukkah party, complete with latkes and spinning dreidels. Or throw religious purism to the

Focusing on activities *the whole family will enjoy is the key to a stress-free holiday season. Continue the traditions you all look forward to and omit those that are simply obligations.*

winds and dub the Christmas tree a "holiday" tree. You may risk confusing the children or raising the grandparents' eyebrows, but at least your immediate family will feel more united over the holidays.

In a family newly blended through divorce and remarriage, deciding whose traditions to follow can be fraught with tension. Maybe your kids have always opened their presents on Christmas Eve, but your new stepchildren always unveil theirs on Christmas morning. To avoid the sense that one family's traditions are prevailing over the other's, perhaps you can agree to open the stockings and a few presents the night before Christmas and save the rest for Christmas Day.

Even in a household of one, it's easy to cling to customs that cause stress. Let's say your college roommate's New Year's

Eve party has evolved from a casual gathering of congenial friends into a chic soiree where dressed-to-kill strangers regale you with accounts of their latest blockbuster business deals. Of course, you could always go to another party or simply stay home, but that might mean sacrificing one of the few times in the year you get to see your friend. Why not suggest that, while you'll skip the party, the two of you declare a new holiday—Procrastinators' New Year—and meet for a champagne brunch one weekend in the middle of January?

A FAMILY AFFAIR

If the holidays always fly by in a haze of hustle, bustle, and good intentions—and later you wonder where they went—do things differently this year: Plan ahead for family time and make a point of taking one or two special excursions together. Around Halloween, go for a drive through

Holiday Portraits

A formal studio portrait of the whole family can be a pricey holiday keepsake. Instead, have everybody take turns shooting snaps as you go about the business of shopping, decorating, and celebrating. Make prints of the best shot of each person, and combine them all in a single frame or mount them in an inexpensive photograph album.

the countryside and buy pumpkins at a farm stand. During the kids' Christmas break, spend a day sledding. Go to an outdoor ice-skating rink for an evening, or take a nighttime tour of your town's most elaborate Christmas decorations; follow up with cookies and hot chocolate at home. When the spring holidays beckon, plan a family wildflower walk or bird-watching adventure. The possibilities are myriad, limited only by your imagination and your family's collective interests.

Holidays are ideal times to sneak in a little learning along with family fun. For instance, holidays celebrating historical figures are natural springboards for hands-on history lessons, whether you visit the National Civil Rights Museum in Memphis, Tennessee, for Martin Luther King Day, or take a trip to George Washington's Mount Vernon over Presidents' Day weekend. Nor do you have to plan an elaborate trip; something as simple as gathering around the kitchen table on Veterans Day as your father-in-law talks about his wartime experiences can add meaning to the holiday.

Many zoos, botanical gardens, planetariums, aquariums, national and state parks, and natural history museums sponsor holiday events. These include all-day field trips, storytelling sessions, classes, and hands-on exhibits. Nature itself may oblige by putting on a show, such as the December whale migration off the California coast or early January's Quadrantid meteor showers. If nothing else, take a walk through the woods or along a wintry beach. Explore the stubbled fields of a nearby farm or a stretch of desert not far

BUSYING LITTLE HANDS

✳

Young children need to feel that they're a part of holiday preparations. You can keep them happy and occupied with simple decorating projects such as these. Have an aunt, an uncle, or a grandparent supervise if you'll be busy with other things.

▲ **Make a "gingerbread" house** *by molding graham crackers and frosting around a milk-carton form.*

▼ **Create holiday "crackers"** *to pop open at parties by filling cardboard tubes with candies and small toys. Wrap them, tie the ends, and add stickers.*

▲ **Trace "gingerbread" men** *on cardboard with cookie cutters. Then cut them out to use as tree decorations.*

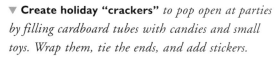

▲ **Make "stained-glass" ornaments** *by cutting a hole in cookie dough, filling it with hard candy, and baking.*

HOLIDAY GETAWAYS

✳

H AS YOUR EXTENDED FAMILY tired of the same old holiday routine? Maybe a new gathering site can help you all relax and enjoy each other while sharing brand-new experiences. Here are a few ideas:

	Good for young kids	Good for older kids	Cost effective	Quick to arrange
Book nights at a YMCA family camp. Often in breathtaking locations, these modestly priced establishments offer year-round activities for all ages. Family-style meals are usually provided, letting you enjoy the holiday without being stuck in the kitchen.	●	●	●	
Take a family cruise. A memorable way to combine adventure with a holiday get-together. Older children especially love the freedom aboard a ship. Activity directors keep things hopping with amusements for all. Cruises can be expensive, however.		●		◐
Stay at an all-inclusive resort. Many resorts cater to families over the holidays, planning activities and meals to celebrate the season. Swimming pools, spas, golf, skiing, and other recreation are often on the grounds. Look for resorts offering all-inclusive deals so you'll know costs up front and can divide them evenly.	●	●		◐
Explore a big city. A big city at holiday time is a magical world of twinkling lights and store windows sprung to life. Choose a centrally located hotel so you can explore the city on foot and stroll to museums, concert halls, and theaters. Many hotels have babysitters who can entertain the little ones for a day.	●	●	◐	◐
Rent a beach house. The ocean is a draw in any season, but winter skies add drama to an already breathtaking landscape. Or take a midwinter trip from cold climates to warm sands—you're almost guaranteed that everyone will be relaxed.	●	●	◐	◐
Go skiing. Skiing is a terrific family activity, and the exercise is just the ticket for working off big holiday meals. Accommodations can range from rustic cabins to resort hotels with all the amenities. If your group includes nonskiers and very young children, choose a resort that offers lots of other activities.	◐	●		◐
Volunteer with a charity. For families with teens or adult children, churches and nonprofit groups sponsor holiday-season mission trips, both abroad and closer to home. Some of these are construction projects or research treks. Housing can be primitive and amenities few, but the rewards are beyond price.		◐	●	◐

from home. See how many birds, fish, mammals, reptiles, trees, and shrubs you can identify—or simply relax and watch the natural world unfold all around you.

BACK TO BASICS

Holidays also provide excellent opportunities to learn more about your own family's heritage or the customs of other ethnic groups. If your family tree includes a bit of the green, take the kids to see Irish step dancers or a Celtic musical group on Saint Patrick's Day. If Nana was from Naples, take the family for a Columbus Day feast at your favorite Italian restaurant. Other holidays also offer wonderful teaching opportunities, whether it's the harvest- and family-oriented traditions of Kwanzaa or

Holidays provide the opportunity to learn more about your family heritage and that of others.

the lion dances and firecrackers of the Chinese New Year. Maybe the neighbors down the block who are Greek Orthodox invite you to join in their sunrise Easter observance, and you return the favor by welcoming them to your Passover seder.

As easy as it is to get carried away by a holiday's commercial trappings, you can furnish perspective by reminding your kids of the date's real significance, religious or otherwise. Has Hanukkah become just a gift fest for your kids? Remind them of its origin celebrating an uprising against religious persecution. Has Christmas become little more than a pile of presents and

FAMILY fun

OLD-FASHIONED AMUSEMENTS ARE STILL HARD TO BEAT WHEN THE FAMILY GATHERS TOGETHER FOR THE HOLIDAYS.

◈

Sing-along books
A book of Christmas carols or other songs is just the thing when everyone's gathered around Grandma's piano.

Picture books
Illustrated holiday stories delight younger children, who love to look at the pictures, and those children who are learning to read.

Jigsaw puzzles
Whether it's the simple kind for toddlers or a tabletop behemoth, a jigsaw puzzle is guaranteed to keep everyone busy.

Board games
Classic board games such as backgammon, chess, and checkers never fail to occupy family members of all ages.

Tops
Adults and children alike appreciate simple, traditional toys such as tops. They give the whole family a chance to play together.

Party masks
Children love to play make-believe. Using a few masks and a trunk of old clothes, they can create an entertaining skit for the adults.

The holidays are a perfect time to practice the art of giving.

glittery decorations? It might be time to discuss the birth of Christ in Bethlehem. Even if you're not religious, reminding children about the spiritual ideal behind Christmas—that feeling of goodwill toward all—can bestow a significance to the season far beyond what Frosty the Snowman or Santa's elves can impart.

GIVING TO OTHERS

Another way to lend real meaning to the holidays is to make helping others part of your celebration. Your choices depend on your kids' ages, your talents and inclinations, and available time, but possibilities abound. You can invite a solitary widowed neighbor over for a festive dinner the kids help prepare, or have the kids offer to shovel that person's driveway. The musically inclined in your family might enjoy being part of the Holiday Project, a group that rallies singers and musicians of any

ability to bring cheer to nursing homes in 25 U.S. cities. If your business allows you to take extended time off over the holidays, there are few more gratifying ways to spend that time than rolling up your sleeves for Habitat for Humanity, a U.S. organization that teams up volunteers with would-be home owners to build low-cost housing.

If your kids are younger, you might volunteer some time as a family at a local food bank, where everyone can help bag groceries, count cans, or organize boxes. Many schools and businesses sponsor toy, clothing, or food drives at Thanksgiving and Christmas—have the kids go through the pantry with you, or take them shopping to pick out items to donate. Encourage kids to go through their closets and toy boxes early in the holiday season, pull out toys they no longer play with or clothes they've outgrown, and give these to charity. At the very least, make sure that your kids see you toss some coins into Salvation Army kettles and Humane Society baskets as you make your holiday shopping rounds. They'll learn by example that donations needn't always be substantial—small gestures are important, too.

Encourage kids to give away the toys they no longer play with and the clothes they've outgrown.

Nor do you have to confine your spirit of giving to the Christmas season. Try applying the spirit of Valentine's Day in the widest sense—make it an annual family tradition for the day. Take flowers or a box of chocolates to strangers in a nursing home. Drive up to the tollbooth on the bridge and pay for your car and the one behind you. Buy some food, toys, and

clothes; bundle everything inside a red-and-white tablecloth; and leave it, no note attached, on the doorstep of a family that's seen some tough times lately. Buy a few packages of native wildflower seeds and scatter the seeds in an ugly vacant lot or beside a rusted chain-link fence.

Or honor Easter and Earth's rebirth by volunteering for a spring cleanup project. If the weather permits, help clear hiking trails at a nearby preserve or collect litter in a neighborhood park. Show the kids that individuals really can make a difference in this world of ours.

HOLIDAY ROMANCE

If you've paid the slightest attention to magazine and TV ads over the years, you know that between Thanksgiving and New Year's every normal adult in the world is supposed to be half of a devoted twosome.

SIMPLE SOLUTIONS

A GIFT FOR EACH OTHER

WHEN THE HOUSE IS FILLED with relatives you haven't seen since the last big family gathering, it's often difficult for you and your spouse to find time for each other. But there are ways you can carve out time together and still be good hosts.

Simple — Send everyone out to a movie or an afternoon at a local theme park or historical site—your treat. You can buy tickets ahead of time, draw up a map, and hand over your car keys to make it easy on your guests.

Simpler — Find a time when everyone seems to be winding down—napping, reading books, watching television—and take a walk or a drive with your spouse. Let your guests know when you'll be returning.

Simplest — Retire to your bedroom an hour earlier than you usually go to sleep. Direct your guests to the television, reading materials, and late-evening snacks before you disappear to your own quarters.

Set aside time
for holiday romance.

These perfect couples spend nearly all their time together, frolicking in the snow, gliding across gleaming dance floors, or simply sitting by the fire gazing into each other's eyes. They part only for as long as it takes to find the perfect gift for each other, enclose it in perfect wrappings, and lay it gently beneath the perfect Christmas tree. Of course, the real world doesn't work that

and your spouse are one of those happy (or at least contented) couples, make the most of it. Try at least once during the season to hire a babysitter and get away by yourselves—for a weekend at a country inn, an evening on the town, or an afternoon of cross-country skiing. Or just send the kids to a slumber party at their cousins' house and spend a quiet evening at home.

Try at least once during the holidays to get away by yourselves—for a weekend at a country inn, a night on the town, or an afternoon of skiing.

way, and for most of the year many of us are just as glad it doesn't. But around major holidays—especially Christmas—even the most independent of us can feel that something's missing from our lives.

If the holidays find you alone and you don't like the feeling, see page 18 for tips on combating the solo blues. But if you

Chill some champagne, order dinner from a restaurant that delivers, and light a fire (not necessarily the kind in the fireplace). Or just snuggle on the sofa and watch a good video—those with happy endings are strongly suggested. If it does nothing else, rekindling your romance at holiday time will fortify you for the season's trials.

THE MORE, THE MERRIER

❋

COMING UP WITH A STRATEGY FOR CELEBRATING WITH YOUR SPOUSE AND CHILDREN DOESN'T HOLD A CANDLE TO THAT OLYMPIC EVENT OF HOLIDAY PLANNING: GETTING TOGETHER WITH YOUR ENTIRE EXTENDED FAMILY.

Like a champion figure skater, you'll need grace under pressure, sheer endurance, a clever routine, and the ability to charm the judges. And if you fall short in any of these areas, don't worry—there's not a family on the planet that skates through the holidays without a few spills, missed jumps, or wobbles on the landing.

FAMILY MATTERS

So far no one has discovered a surefire way of taking the stress out of large family gatherings. You might be able to get everyone to sit still and say "cheese" for the ritual group snapshot—and their expressions might seem serene and composed—but the minute the flash goes off, the kids are off racing their ride-'em fire trucks down the hall. Aunt Marie is gathering up pieces of wrapping paper to save for next year. The teenagers split to go off somewhere on their own. And you're pacing the floor because, according to your calculations, the turkey should have been done an hour ago even though the meat thermometer says it's rare. Ah, family bliss.

As always, your best weapons in the battle against mayhem are advance negotiations, preparation, an easygoing attitude, and a sense of humor. Be especially aware of the logistical demands of holiday travel and sensitive to the toll that long

trips take on your family. Maybe blasting through gift opening on Christmas morning, then driving two hours in nasty traffic for a lunchtime buffet at your in-laws', followed by a full Christmas dinner with your folks back home isn't the best way to celebrate the holiday. To spend a decent amount of time with everyone, consider postponing at least one of your family get-togethers until summer. Even if the living isn't exactly easy, at least the kids are out of school for a longer time, your year-end business meetings are behind you, and it's highly unlikely you'll be caught in a blizzard on your way to Grandma's.

Putting It All Together

Set up a card table with a jig-saw puzzle for guests to work on during lulls in the action. Assembling a jigsaw puzzle is a great way to bring family members of all ages together. Take a picture of the finished product, and have extra copies made to give to everyone who labored over the magnum opus.

When you anticipate opposition or clashes in traditions, discuss the situation as early and as openly as possible. Recognize that it may take a while for your family to get used to different routines and new ideas, and try to encourage your relatives to give you constructive feedback as they become accustomed to the changes.

THE BIG GET-TOGETHER

When it's your turn to host the extended family during the holidays, whether at Thanksgiving or for an Easter brunch, a bit of advance planning will help ensure a good time for all. Consider everyone's ages and interests and try to have some activities on hand that will make the time go by pleasantly. Games can be very helpful here. Lay in a supply of popular board

If you plan your holiday gatherings well in advance and give your guests plenty of notice, everyone will be relaxed and able to enjoy one another at the big event.

games like Scrabble, checkers, Risk, and Parcheesi. Science museums, mail-order catalogs, and game stores sell elegant three-dimensional puzzles that will keep everyone from your six-year-old to your sister the physicist engrossed for hours. To produce surefire laughs, whip out a couple of those fill-in-the-blank books that ask you to sprinkle random nouns, verbs, and adjectives into a story to comic effect. It will help out when frayed nerves or boredom threatens to dampen the festivities. Play charades, or mix kids and adults on teams for a neighborhood scavenger hunt. (See page 136 for additional ideas.)

If weather permits, let children work off some of their energy tossing a ball outside, jumping rope, or flying kites. But if the weather's bad and the kids are really antsy, maybe someone could ferry them to a movie, an indoor play gym, a bowling alley, or a video arcade for a couple of hours while you put the finishing touches on dinner. And don't forget to schedule a

little downtime—a stock of popular videos and reading materials can help young and old take a break during the day (see pages 134 and 135 for suggested titles).

LONG VISITS

There are those among us who seem to find true happiness only when every bed in the house is spoken for and the dining room fills up at mealtimes like the most popular restaurant in town.

For the rest of us, though, coping with temporary household expansion is a challenge, no matter how closely the visitors are related to us or how much we may enjoy their company under less intimate—or less prolonged—circumstances. Once everyone gets past those first greetings,

When it's your turn to host the extended family, try to have some activities on hand that will make the time go by pleasantly.

discussions of the latest family news, and guided tours of the kids' toy boxes, what do you do to keep everyone amused, occupied, and out of your hair while you get on with holiday preparations?

For starters, let them help. Suppose your mother suggests that she whip up her famous pumpkin cheesecake with gingersnap crust. Accept with thanks. (So what if you were planning to make mincemeat pie? You can do that another time.) If your brother offers to run errands while he's out for his morning jog, hand him your Christmas cards and ask him to drop

Jingle Toes

Tie bells to the shoes of toddlers or babies who are just starting to walk. They'll love the sound the bells make—just walking around the house will keep them entertained. You'll always know where they are, even if you're stuck cooking at the stove or cleaning the bathroom. And the bells will add a festive holiday sound to your home.

them in the mailbox as he runs past the corner. You can probably find a willing hand for almost everything else as well, from polishing the silver to tending bar.

Well before your houseguests arrive, spend time mulling over their hobbies, interests, and careers so you can plan some compatible activities. Take your father, the retired third baseman. You and your kids have heard his repertoire of stories so many times you know each one by heart. But you can bet that 10-year-old baseball historian down the street would give her last Mickey Mantle card for a chance to hear his tales. Send the two of them out for lunchtime burgers and sodas (if there's a nearby diner plastered with sports memorabilia, you've struck pay dirt).

Cast your mind in the right direction and you'll find matchmaking possibilities everywhere: Introduce your needlepoint-loving cousin to the people at the local yarn shop. Call your friend the gourmet food writer and ask if she'd like to meet your sister the chef from New Orleans. Once you introduce them, let your guests and their new friends take it from there.

If your guests are new to your area, build in time to show them the sights—or enlist a less frantic family member to act as tour guide. Use the local paper or city magazine, a savvy guidebook, or Internet

A visit to the House of the Seven Gables or some other nearby literary landmark might just make her day.

When you're exploring the local attractions, don't overlook churches, even if you aren't religious. In many towns they offer some of the best architecture—and acoustics—you'll find. From Thanksgiving day through the Feast of the Epiphany on

Gather a list of holiday attractions and events: concerts, plays, local parades. Let your guests' interests be your guide.

services to help you gather a list of holiday attractions and events: concerts, plays, places of historical interest, museum exhibits, local parades and pageants. Let your guests' interests be your guide. Is Uncle Larry a custom-car buff? A ticket for the annual auto show might be just the thing. Is Great-Aunt Mary an avid gardener? A tour of the local nurseries during Holy Week would occupy her happily for hours. College sophomore Courtney can't get enough of early American Gothic writers?

January 6, they're filled with stirring music and festive decorations. For those who like to sing (and who doesn't?), the Sing-It-Yourself *Messiah*—a holiday tradition in several U.S. cities—makes a wonderful excursion. For the price of admission, you join others (in a group as large as thousands) for an impromptu performance of Handel's choral masterpiece.

Of course, some people seem born to the role of houseguest—they pitch in with chores, play with the kids, and entertain

Liven up your get-together
with exciting group activities.

themselves. These people tend to find adventure wherever they go. All you need to do is stock a few guidebooks, event calendars, and a copy of the local newspaper, and they will amuse themselves for days. Show them your gratitude by being a good houseguest when it's your turn to visit.

Finally, even if you did enough strategic planning to make Napoleon envious—and your relatives still had a disappointing time at the outdoor Fourth of July concert (the lawn was too damp), your five-year-old broke her arm during the family's ice-skating outing over Christmas, or you found out that Grandpa Abel is allergic to honey after he ate a piece of your homemade baklava and broke out in hives—don't give up. Retreat to that quiet, peaceful place in your mind and take several deep breaths. Fine-tune your strategy, be flexible, and remember that, for all their complaints and idiosyncrasies, your relatives still offer a sense of belonging and mutual love that's worth a few gray hairs.

STAYING IN TOUCH

So far we've focused on the people we'll actually carve a turkey with or kiss under the mistletoe. But what about the friends and family members you aren't able to visit in person during the holidays? How do you stay in touch with them?

Some people just have a knack for maintaining long-term, long-distance relationships: the woman who flies 3,000 miles to attend the medical-school graduation of the son of her best friend from kindergarten; the man who has worked in 35 towns on four continents but who still

Far Away Together

If your family is spread far and wide, start a seasonal ritual that everyone follows wherever they are—baking heart-shaped cakes, waving sparklers, dyeing Easter eggs. Take a snapshot and send copies to the whole group, or just get on the phone and talk about your adventures. You'll have a sense of belonging even though you're miles apart.

keeps up with half his colleagues; the couple who still vacation with people they met on their honeymoon in 1947. How do they do it when other people, once they've moved away, have trouble merely staying in touch with their siblings?

The answer is natural inclination and a lot of perseverance. Even if you lack the former and are a wee bit wanting in the latter, the holidays—especially the winter ones—bring a special gift: a chance to re-enter the fold of old friendships and renew lapsed family ties. The evidence suggests that all the time, trouble, and expense of writing cards are well worth it: Recent psychological studies show that people who receive Christmas, Hanukkah, or New Year's cards—even from casual acquaintances—experience increased feelings of self-esteem and connection to others.

Additional research associates this feeling of connectedness with better health and longer life. In other words, reaching

EASY GREETINGS

✳

MAILBOXES ARE PACKED WITH HOLIDAY cards and party invitations toward the end of the year. With a little imagination, you can make yours stand out from the crowd without spending much time or money. Here are a few simple ideas.

▲ **Have your kids** *draw holiday scenes and affix them to note cards.*

◀ **Slip a favorite photo** *under a sheet of translucent paper tied to a card. Write your greeting directly on the paper.*

▲ **Create festive** *hand-delivered invitations by attaching peppermint sticks and ribbons.*

▲ **Write a** *New Year's invite on the back of a mask and toss confetti in the envelope.*

out and touching someone is not only a nice thing to do—it's good for you and for your friends and relatives.

So If you can't visit in person, make the connection by sending a letter or card. If you have a list of friends, relatives, acquaintances, and business colleagues a mile long, you can find ways to simplify the annual rite: Simply sign your name and put a one-line wish for happy holidays on cards destined for the last two categories, and make more of an effort for those who hold a special place in your heart.

That effort can mean buying your cards in the beginning of November and writing a personal note on a few each day until you've covered everyone on your list. If your children are old enough, maybe you can divvy up the writing duties in the family, with everyone handling a batch in his or her own personal style. If you're not tied to the idea of the handwritten note, your computer can be a big help in sending holiday cheer—and no, we're not talking about those three-page, single-spaced group letters detailing everything from your big raise in September to your son's victory in the soccer tournament. It's fine to start with a boilerplate letter covering some of last year's highlights, but it really means a lot to people if you customize the letter for each recipient.

Sending e-mail greetings is becoming a popular alternative (some online services will even provide the appropriate seasonal graphics). Or pick a time and date for your long-distance friends and family members to gather in your own holiday online chat room. If you have a scanner, you can send

Wishing You a Happy New Year

If, no matter how hard you try, you can't get Christmas cards in the mail even in time for the champagne corks to pop on New Year's Eve, don't fret. Instead, send New Year's cards in mid-January. That way you can spend more time on personal messages, and your friends will likely have more time to read them.

pictures of your children and yourself whizzing through cyberspace, or even set up your own family holiday Web page.

REACHING OUT

For relatives and close friends, you might consider sending audio greetings instead of cards. Record the kids singing songs, reciting poems, or reading stories about Christmas, Hanukkah, or Kwanzaa, then duplicate and mail the tapes. Or you might shoot a day-in-the-life video of your family and send duplicates to grandparents or neighbors you've left behind.

If chatting on the telephone is your thing, set up conference calls with distant pals—most phone providers now offer three-way calling that works from home just as it does at the office. The point is, thanks to the high-tech revolution in all its many forms, there are more ways than ever to send season's greetings to all your dear ones, far and near.

SIMPLIFYING holiday
Trimmings

—✳—

1 Decide how much decorating you want to do for each **holiday** your family celebrates. **2** Do as much decorating as your time and **inclination** call for, and let it go at that. **3** If you're decorating for Christmas and time is at a premium, decorate only the **room** your family uses most often. **4** When you have time to spare, invest it in weeding out the **decorations** you no longer use. **5** Decide on an **approach,** whether it's reusing last year's decorations or building a new look around a theme or color. **6** Take advantage of basic **design** rules to achieve a decorating theme with real impact. **7** Learn some of the tricks that professional decorators use to achieve maximum **effect** with minimum effort. **8** Assemble a **"wardrobe"** of decorative elements, such as grapevine wreaths and terra-cotta pots, that you can use to create **atmosphere** for any holiday. **9** Use items from a **collection,** such as dolls or teddy bears, as the foundation of your holiday decor. ●

HOLIDAY DECORATING

SIMPLE ADORNMENTS THAT
ENHANCE THE SEASON

——————*

For most people, decking the house in its seasonal finery—while it ranks among life's great pleasures—can be an exercise in executive decision making, diplomacy, and time management. Do you build your decor around a theme or just haul all the decorations out of the closet? What do you do if some members of your family celebrate Christmas and others celebrate Hanukkah or Kwanzaa? And how do you decorate for other holidays—Valentine's Day, Easter, the Fourth of July—if you barely even have time to celebrate them?

Relax. With a few basic decisions, a little organization—and some sleight of hand—you can make your home convey a festive welcome to visitors and give you and your children wonderful memories to carry through the years. And you can do it all without taking a sabbatical from your full-time job or putting an interior decorator on retainer.

DECKING THE HALLS

———— ✳ ————

Winter holiday decorating is a joy for many but creates a sea-sonal quandary for others: Faced with a blank canvas called home, how do you decide how much to do—or even where to begin?

And when members of your family celebrate different holidays—Christmas, Hanukkah, Kwanzaa—how do you decorate in a way that's appropriate to all celebrations? There's no right or wrong way to approach the matter. Just do what seems the fairest, the least stressful—and the most joyful—for all concerned.

Every family has its traditions, but there's no question that Christmas is the most decor-intensive holiday of all. After all, the only trappings traditionally associated with Hanukkah are the menorah and

Elaborating on a favorite *theme makes holiday decorating easier. This collection of wooden nutcrackers enhanced with holiday greenery creates a simple yet festive display.*

perhaps a dreidel or two. Similarly, Kwanzaa is built around simple tokens: a straw place mat, the seven-candled kinara, the communal unity cup, ears of corn, fruits and vegetables, and small gifts.

But as complex as Christmas decorating often becomes, you can easily de-stress it. The first step comes with banishing the demons of perfection that haunt so many people during the festive season. You don't have to do it all, and you don't have to do any of it perfectly. Decide what makes sense for you this year and take it from there. If time is less plentiful than usual this holiday season, concentrate on the room where your family spends most of its time and forget the rest. Stick to the basics, the elements without which no one

in your family would consider it Christmas. If that means a tree, by all means have one, and decorate it any way that suits your fancy. But If everyone would just as soon string chili-pepper lights on the potted cactus in the corner, that'll do just fine. After all, this is your celebration.

On the other hand, if you do have a little time to spare this season, some extra work could result in simpler, more festive times this year and in years to come. Before the Christmas rush starts, get rid of any decorations you haven't used in the last two years and know you never will—the plastic holly with dust embedded in its leaves, the glow-in-the-dark snowman you won as a door prize at the office party, the plaster Rudolph with the fiber-optic nose that makes you cringe. Next, set aside anything you genuinely treasure that's been damaged—the broken crystal ornaments that need only a touch of glue, the wide taffeta bows that would look elegant on

Purchase an ornament box *for your fragile heirloom ornaments. Year after year, you'll know they're safe from breakage.*

ornament boxes or the rigid plastic, sealable kinds meant to hold sweaters. When the holidays are over, wrap fragile ornaments carefully in paper or bubble wrap and tuck them gently away. Any that are made of fabric or paper should be wrapped in acid-free tissue and stored in an acid-free box, available at most large craft stores and

If you'd just as soon string lights on the potted cactus in the corner, that's fine. After all, this is your celebration.

the stair rail if you starched and ironed them, the silk-and-velvet crazy-quilt stocking with a hole in its toe. Attend to them this year or give them to somebody who will. If the decoration is priceless and you lack the time or ability to do the repair yourself, have a pro tackle the job.

Long before you take down the Christmas tree, invest in plenty of packing materials and sturdy containers—if you wait till after the holidays, you may not find any left. Look for either the specially designed

through mail-order catalogs. Label each container and keep it in a cool, dry, ventilated spot where there's no risk of the boxes and their fragile contents being damaged. (See page 141 for a cleanup checklist.)

FINDING YOUR STYLE

There are as many approaches to holiday decorating as there are holiday decorators. Some people choose one method and stick with it for life; others vary their technique from year to year depending on available

THE FALL PRELUDE

---✳---

WITH THE WINTER REVELRIES APPROACHING, there's every rea-son to keep Halloween and Thanksgiving decorations simple. To achieve easy effects like these, you need look no farther than your nearest craft store and the local pumpkin patch.

▲ **String a clothesline** *in a hallway or living room to display pinecones and dried flowers and leaves.*

◀ **Greet trick-or-treaters** *with a ghostly group of handkerchiefs or napkins tied around small balls and hung from a tree outside your door.*

▲ **An arrangement** *of apples and dried flowers is easy to make. Use toothpicks to attach the fruit to a cone of florist's foam.*

▲ **A few pumpkins** *and gourds surrounded by dried flowers and grasses celebrate autumn's bounty with warmth and simplicity.*

time, the nature of the year's festivities, or simply the whim of the moment. Here are some tried-and-true options:

Do it the same way every year This is the only approach that wins the full approval of young children, who firmly believe that nothing should ever change, especially when it comes to holidays. It also greatly simplifies life for adults, who

Let a theme or color be your guide: Follow the lead of favorite tree ornaments or an heirloom quilt.

don't have to make decisions: The same things go in the same places. Some come out of storage boxes—glass-ball ornaments and silvery garlands, for example. Others you buy afresh each year—poinsettias for the mantel top and a fresh pine wreath for the door. And since you always know what you want, you can shop early, easily and in quantity—even order everything by phone if you want to.

Pick a favorite theme. This method is popular with collectors, who build holiday decorating schemes around their treasures, whether they be teddy bears, Victoriana, angels, antique toys, folk art animals, or sophisticated contemporary crafts such as blown-glass vases. Some people stick with one theme year after year but vary specific elements as their collections grow; others change subject matter from one Christmas to the next. This is a wonderful approach for the kind of person who is at once a passionate collector and a devotee of calm, uncluttered surroundings. You can buy

teddy bears, let's say, to your heart's content, keep them tucked away for most of the year, then bring them out in all their glory for the holiday season.

How far you go with the theme is strictly up to you. You can start small—for instance, three bears with red ribbons around their necks, grouped in a red wagon under the tree. Meanwhile, begin a quest for bear tree ornaments and add a few every year. Most likely it will be a while before your collection covers the tree, but in the meantime you can fill in with lots of white lights and red bows.

Build on a color scheme. Let color be your guide: Follow the lead of favorite tree ornaments or an heirloom quilt, and let your imagination take it from there. The effect is usually elegant and always more restrained than the haul-out-everything-in-the-box-and-hang-it-on-the-tree approach. Like the method of doing everything the

Friendly Crafts

Throughout the year, craft shops, nurseries, and botanical gardens offer classes in wreath-making and other holiday crafts. Check your local paper for dates, then call a couple of friends you've been wanting to see and sign up together. You'll spend a day in congenial company, learn a new skill, and come away with lovely handmade decorations.

Personal Trees

If your ornament collection has outgrown your tree, or if some ornaments clash with this year's theme, put small trees in each of the children's rooms and let them choose the trimmings they want (heirlooms not included). That way, you can control which ornaments go on the main tree without sending anyone's favorites back to storage.

candleholders, add a few red balls to the grouping on the mantel, hang some more red balls from the tree, and presto—you have an entirely new look.

UNUSUAL SOURCES

Decorate with kids' crafts. This can be a good approach if you have young children who enjoy crafts and like to be kept busy over the holidays. Depending on their ages, talents, and inclinations, they could make papier-mâché Santa Clauses, cut out snowflakes for the windows, or weave yarn place mats for your holiday table. Don't despair if your early efforts fall short of the mark. For instance, if you and the kids set out to make bread-dough ornaments and the net results consist of a cut finger, a couple of broken bowls, and a dozen soggy beige rocking horses, chalk it up to experience. Take everybody to the neighborhood bakery and buy lots of gingerbread men to hang on the tree (handmade doesn't have to mean *you* made it). There's also no rule that says you can't cover the tree with hand-tied bows and candy canes.

same way every year, this one simplifies life by narrowing choices—when you go shopping, you know you want silver ribbon, a white tree skirt, or gold metallic cord.

The one-color approach is also good for those who like a bit of change every year, because even a few small dashes of another color make for a striking impact. Let's say that one year you have an all-white Christmas, with white ornaments

Make liberal use of organic materials—evergreen trees and boughs, fruits, nuts, pinecones, flowers, even driftwood logs and fallen tree limbs.

and lights on the tree, white azaleas in white pottery pots scattered around the room, a vintage cutwork tablecloth as a tree skirt, white blown-glass balls nestled in pine boughs on the mantel, and white tapers in white pottery candleholders. The next year, you use a red-and-white checkered tablecloth for the tree skirt, tie red ribbons around the azalea pots and

The handmade theme also works well if you've got talented friends and relatives who are generous enough to give you the fruits of their labors. Encourage them—perhaps by making a tradition of exchanging handmade decorations at Christmas.

Let nature provide the decor. Modern or old-fashioned in tone, the natural look makes liberal use of organic materials such as evergreen trees and boughs, fruits, nuts, pinecones, flowers both fresh and dried, even driftwood logs and fallen tree limbs. This can be a cost-saving approach to decorating, not to mention a lot of fun both coming and going: You can gather materials on beach walks or mountain hikes, in your garden or favorite produce market. And what can't be stored away for next year can be eaten, composted, shredded into mulch for the garden, or burned in the fireplace on cold winter nights.

INSTANT IMPACT

If the sugarplums in your dreams far outnumber the hours in your day, don't despair—and don't knock yourself out. Make a few simple gestures instead and leave yourself time to sit back and enjoy the results. Here are some ideas whose impact will far outweigh the effort that's required to put them into effect.

After a storm, collect fallen evergreen branches, rinse off any debris, cut them to size, and put them in vases—the bigger the display the better, but even tiny sprigs in bud vases will look and smell festive. You can also hang small glass balls on the branches or tie red bows on the vases or greenery for a touch of color.

For a knockout effect in almost no time, buy half a dozen red amaryllis flowers (you'll find these striking plants, potted and blooming, in the florist section of any large supermarket at Christmastime) and place them artfully around the room. Buy more if you want, or fewer—in a small room even one makes a big impact.

There's no need to get all tangled up in an elaborate decorating scheme.

Saving for Christmas Future

Give your kids a head start on holiday decorating. Buy them each a special storage box, and each year give them an ornament—a family heirloom or a piece you've made by hand or chosen carefully—to put away for the future. When they have their own homes, they'll have tree trimmings of their own, too.

Outdoors, nail a store-bought wreath to the door, or use an over-the-door hanger from a houseware store or mail-order catalog. Or tie a ribbon around the lamppost and line the porch steps with red and pink poinsettias (weather permitting).

Even when it seems there's no time at all, there are still ways to give your surroundings instant holiday cheer. Try displaying some of the following:

- WHITE BOWLS FILLED WITH ANYTHING RED—CRANBERRIES, APPLES, CANDY
- POTS, VASES, OR CANDLESTICKS TIED WITH RED OR GOLD RIBBONS
- HOLIDAY CARDS PILED IN A WICKER BASKET TIED WITH A BIG BOW

When the minutes are galloping by and guests are about to arrive on your doorstep, summon your greatest ally: aroma. Scent is the most powerful mood-inducer of all, and it takes very little to say "Season's Greetings" loud and clear. Slice up a roll of refrigerated gingerbread cookie dough and pop a trayful into the oven. Pour a bottle of red wine and a packet of mulling spices into a stockpot and keep it simmering on the stove. Or toss orange rind and whatever sweet spices you have on hand—cinnamon, cloves, nutmeg, ginger—into a pot, cover them with water, bring to a boil, and then simmer.

O CHRISTMAS TREE

People tend to have strong feelings about Christmas trees—about which kind to buy and how to decorate it, or even whether to have a tree at all. When you're trying to simplify holiday celebrations, there's no doubt about it: Artificial trees have certain advantages. There are many kinds to choose from, and most are better-looking than they used to be. Buying one will save you from having to shop for a tree every year or vacuum pine needles from your carpet. (If you have dust allergies, be sure to vacuum the tree before storing it away.) If your desire for an artificial tree stems from environmental concerns, however, bear in mind that the cut and live trees sold commercially are grown on farms, not taken from the forest, old-growth or otherwise. So buying a cut Christmas tree is not a whole lot different from buying a dozen ears of corn, provided you dispose of it thoughtfully at the end of the season.

For many of us, the annual trek to find the "perfect tree" is an adventure without which no Christmas would be complete. Make the quest easier by adjusting your idea of perfection: So what if the chosen specimen has irregularities? Few things are more boring than flawless symmetry.

TRIMMING THE TREE

——— ✳ ———

WHEN TREE-TRIMMING TIME ROLLS AROUND, there's no need to restrict yourself to the familiar tinsel and shiny glass balls. Here are some simple yet clever alternatives that will make your conifer stand out from the crowd.

▲ **Little shoes** *tied to a limb of the tree can adorn your baby's or toddler's feet after the holidays are over.*

▲ **Colorful bags** *of jelly beans will be popular with kids both during and after the holidays.*

▼ **Family photographs** *make heartwarming ornaments. Glue them to colorful paper shapes.*

▲ **Tie silk flowers** *to the branches of your tree using florist's wire. Or attach fresh flowers in water-filled florist's vials.*

There is no "best" kind of tree to buy. If cost and longevity are crucial factors, look for white or Scotch pine. These trees are the most popular and often the least expensive varieties, and they're widely available. If you get one when it's fresh, it should last close to a month. Bend some of the needles: If they're pliable, the tree is fresh. If you have a large collection of hefty ornaments, a Colorado blue spruce might be your best bet; it's among the strongest evergreens you can find—though you'll have to put up with its sharp needles. Balsam and Fraser fir also are sturdy enough to support ornaments securely—and they're very fragrant—but they're often hard to find.

A TREE THAT FITS

Whether you're looking for a tree with particular attributes or simply the prettiest one on the lot, before you start on your quest, measure the height of your ceiling from the floor or from the table your tree will stand on, and subtract the height of whatever will go on top. Then measure the inside diameter of your tree stand. Write it all down on a slip of paper, or in that small notebook you started (see page 22).

To avoid the frustration of a prematurely balding tree—and the hassle of frequent vacuuming—try to buy your tree from a lot or nursery that keeps them standing in water. More and more places are discovering this technique for keeping trees fresh longer. If your prize has been sitting high and dry, put it in water when you get home. But first, cut off an inch or so from the bottom of the trunk (a straight cut, not slanted). This opens the capillaries in the trunk so the tree will absorb water more readily. Keep the tree soaking until you are ready to bring it indoors. If the

---

THE PERFECT TREE—FAST

IT'S YOUR FIRST CHRISTMAS ON YOUR OWN, you don't have an ornament to your name, and you're throwing a holiday party tomorrow night. You want a great-looking, real Christmas tree when your guests arrive. What do you do?

Simple Pick up a tree and purchase dozens of identical ornaments, such as silver or red balls, and one color of lights. You'll avoid time-consuming decisions about where to put everything on the tree.

Simpler Buy the tree but skip the ornaments—just buy lots of lights of a single color or different colors. It should take you less than an hour to string lights on your tree, but the effect is stunning.

Simplest Go to a year-round nursery or a large supermarket and buy a pretrimmed tabletop tree. Many of these are live, so if you take care of them they may be around for several Christmases to come.

Simple decorations can turn a lackluster tree into a showstopper.

weather permits, hose off the needles and branches first—or just give the tree a good shake before you bring it inside—to remove loose needles and other debris.

Have the tree stand ready in an area away from heaters and the fireplace. Once the trunk is set firmly in place, pour in as much water as the stand will hold. You can add a floral preservative at this stage (available wherever you buy cut flowers); although not all experts are convinced it really helps, it certainly can't hurt. This simple recipe has proved effective for cut flowers: Mix 1 part nondiet lemon-lime soda with 3 parts water. For each quart (1L), add $\frac{1}{4}$ teaspoon household bleach.

The acid in the soda improves water flow into the tree, and the bleach reduces the growth of bacteria and fungi. Be sure the water reservoir is always full.

When the holiday is over, check carefully for any hidden ornaments before you bid the tree farewell. If you can, recycle your tree. Many communities arrange for trees to be picked up from sidewalks in front of houses, or from centrally located collection points, and then ground into mulch. If your town doesn't offer this service, rent a chipper and throw a mulch-making block party. Or cut the branches from your tree and use them to protect tender garden plants from winter cold.

If you have a large collection of hefty ornaments, try a Colorado blue spruce. It's one of the strongest evergreens you can find.

If your heart is set on a living tree—complete with pot and soil—go for it. But remember: Keeping it alive after the holidays is not a simple procedure if you live in a cold climate. It may be all but impossible if temperatures are cold enough to freeze the root ball in its container. Even in milder regions, you'll need to do some planning if you want your tree to become a permanent member of your garden.

The easiest way to have a living tree year after year is to select a variety small enough to thrive outdoors in a large pot and keep it on a wheeled plant caddie so you can move it in and out every year. Any living tree temporarily camped indoors must be kept cool and well watered. Place it in the coolest spot in the house, and cover the soil frequently with ice cubes. The ice will keep the soil cool and automatically water the tree as it melts. No

Hanging mistletoe *in a well-traveled spot is an easy way to encourage mirth and festivity. Ornaments and bows are optional.*

matter how carefully you tend a living tree, it should stay indoors no more than two weeks. Then reacclimate it to the outdoors by keeping it in an unheated but sheltered spot for a couple of weeks.

A KISSING BALL

If floor space is at a premium, bring a traditional English touch to your holiday decor: Make a kissing ball to hang from the ceiling. This symbol of rebirth in winter consists of a sphere of greenery—including mistletoe, holly, and ivy—and the

Join together two galvanized-wire basket planters to form a sphere. Line the ribs with greens and hang mistletoe from the bottom.

rules are the same as they are for mistletoe: Whoever stands beneath it has to kiss.

Begin by joining together two galvanized-wire basket planters (the half-round, hanging type sold at garden centers) to form a sphere. Secure the joint by entwining it with wire and then wrapping the seam in many spots with florist's tape. If you like, use wire cutters to remove some of the longitudinal wires and open up the frame for an airier look.

Choose your greens—pine, fir, spruce, eucalyptus or magnolia leaves, holly, ivy, or any combination thereof will all work fine. Using more wire and sprigs of the appropriate length, gather the stems at the top and wire them along the frame to meet at the bottom. Then tie a ribbon bow to the top of the ball to serve as a hanger. At the bottom, tie a smaller bow and hang a sprig of mistletoe from it. If you like, you can hang ornaments or fruit around the sphere. Suspend the result in a door or hallway that's convenient for kissing.

HOLIDAY SAFETY

In the midst of the festive bustle, it's easy to forget that holidays pose hidden dangers for children and pets. Take some simple precautions to avoid tears, regrets, and trips to the emergency room.

The Christmas tree poses some of the greatest dangers. Not only is it tempting to a would-be climber, but all that glittery stuff on it also looks absolutely scrumptious. If you're a kitten, puppy, or baby, those cords and twinkly lights, as well as ornaments, tinsel, ribbons, and wire ornament hangers all shout "Chew me!" And they all can be lethal if they wind up in small throats or stomachs. Keep puppies and kittens out of the holiday room unless they're closely supervised. The simplest way to keep toddlers safe is to put the tree in a corner and block it off with baby gates. When the lights are on, your child will find the scene just as enchanting from a distance as it is up close.

Beware of other decorations. Most Christmas plants are poisonous to humans and animals. Azaleas, holly, ivy, and mistletoe should all be kept out of the reach of anyone tempted to treat them as edibles. The same goes for fallen berries, which look just like candy. And if there's a canine in the house, watch out for *real* candy: A large bar of dark chocolate can make a big dog sick or even kill a small one.

LIVING decorations

LIVE GREENERY CAN BRING HOLIDAY CHEER THROUGHOUT THE HOUSE. DISPLAY THESE PLANTS AS ACCENTS OR CENTERPIECES.

◇

Topiary wreaths

Wreaths of ivy (right) and fragrant thyme (center), trained around wire frames, can go from year-round houseplants to Christmas centerpieces if you decorate them with colorful bows or small ornaments. Hide their plastic or terra-cotta pots by setting the plants in attractive baskets.

Standards

Rosemary (center) and ficus (left) take the shape of miniature trees when their woody stems are twined to form central trunks. Ornaments or even tiny lights can turn these into holiday focal points. You can even cut sprigs of the rosemary to flavor the stuffing for your holiday turkey.

Color accents

Miniature red roses offer a vivid dash of Christmas cheer; given enough light, they'll bloom through Valentine's Day and beyond. Sun-loving cacti with colorful grafts can add a Southwestern flair to your holiday decor. White Phalaenopsis orchids provide a stately counterpoint to holiday glitz and glitter; keep them moist, in filtered light. And you can never go wrong with poinsettias—their coloring was made for Christmas. Some varieties come in pink and gold as well.

DECORATIONS FOR
ALL SEASONS

———————✳———————

S OME PEOPLE HAVE A GIFT FOR PLAYING EACH HOLIDAY TO THE HILT. AS
THE MONTHS PROGRESS, THEIR HOMES GO FROM RESEMBLING A SUGARPLUM
CASTLE TO A FRILLY WALK-IN VALENTINE TO A SETTING FROM *PETER RABBIT*.

Other people take the opposite approach: Once the Christmas tree comes down, the rest of the year just rolls on by. Then there are those in the middle—probably most of us—who would create seasonal touches if only it didn't take so much time. Here's the good news: It doesn't have to. With a few simple materials, you can quickly pull together a decorating scheme for any holiday.

The first step is gathering a collection of props you can mix and match. Some inexpensive supplies can form a blank canvas for all your holiday decorating.

Baskets. A collection of baskets is one of the most useful—and least expensive—decorating investments you can make. Not only are they equally attractive in their natural state or adorned with holiday trimmings—they are also perfect repositories for anything you want to show off or conceal with style. At Easter time you can display your hand-painted blown eggs in a big open basket on the coffee table. The open basket can go on to hold a collection of red, white, and blue marbles for the Fourth of July; miniature pumpkins for Halloween; and red glass hearts on Valentine's Day. Baskets can conceal the plastic pots of your supermarket plants, hold heaps of Thanksgiving gourds or Halloween candy,

It doesn't take much
decorating to create
that holiday magic.

or carry hors d'oeuvres to a New Year's Eve party. You can pick up very attractive baskets for less than a dollar at thrift shops and flea markets, or you can spend hundreds of dollars for an artisan-made one in a craft store or gallery.

THE BASICS

White candles. The white candle is the decorative equivalent of a woman's little black dress. It's sophisticated. It's never out of style or out of place. And with a simple change of accessories, you've got a whole new look. White candles work just as well in your great-grandmother's silver candelabra as they do in your collection of ceramic candlesticks in the shapes of hearts, leprechauns, Easter bunnies, pumpkins,

> **The white candle is the decorative equivalent of the little black dress: It's sophisticated and never out of style or place.**

turkeys, and Santa Clauses. Even if you like to match candle colors to the mood of the holiday at hand, it's a good idea to stock up on white ones—both tapers and votives—whenever you find them on sale. That way you'll be ready for any kind of emergency, from an impromptu dinner party to an unpredicted windstorm that cuts off your electricity.

White ceramic ware. Never equate white with boring. A table set with white plates can go from sophisticated to casual, or from Thanksgiving dinner to Easter brunch, with as little effort as it takes to

Safe and Colorful

Even nontoxic egg dye could give a curious toddler a tummy ache. For a safer alternative, use any of these added to 1 cup (250ml) of boiling water and 1 tablespoon of vinegar: fresh beets or cranberries for pink, yellow onion skins for orange, turmeric for yellow, spinach for green, and canned blueberries or red cabbage leaves for blue.

change the centerpiece. With a stash of white pitchers, bowls, candlesticks, and platters, you've got a bare canvas of holiday decorations in the making.

Terra-cotta pots. Classic unglazed flowerpots, plain or decorated, share many of the advantages of baskets. They're almost as versatile, providing venues for serving or displaying anything from a Mother's Day azalea to an iced bottle of champagne on New Year's Eve (just be sure to use a pot with no drainage hole). And their prices vary just as greatly, from a fraction of a dollar for a tiny flowerpot (buy several dozen to hold white tapers) to hundreds of dollars for a giant hand-thrown urn.

Grapevine wreaths. Wreaths aren't just for Christmas. One of the handiest staples for almost any holiday—and one you can find at any craft store—is a grapevine wreath. Even unadorned, its thick, twined, dark-brown branches look stunning hung on a door. Add a few simple trimmings,

Your collection of antique *glass bottles can add a sentimental touch to Mother's Day by holding a variety of flowers. Group them together for the effect of a large bouquet.*

and it delivers the greetings of almost any season. Tuck in some spring flowers, and it says "Happy Easter" or even "Happy Mother's Day." Weave red and white ribbons among the vines, slip in some paper hearts, and you've got a Valentine's Day welcome hanging on your door. Tie on paper flags for the Fourth of July or dried autumn leaves for Thanksgiving.

THE TRIMMINGS

Once you've assembled even a small collection of baskets, pots, or wreaths, a few trimmings are all you need to turn them into holiday-specific decorations.

Ribbon. Buy basic colors in bulk when you find them on sale: red, white, green, blue, yellow, pink, and orange will take you through every holiday in the calendar.

If you want, stock up on a selection of pastels for spring holidays, but it's not really necessary—green, yellow, pink, and orange entwined with white will do just fine. Twist lengths of blue ribbon around a big white casserole, fill it with pots of bright red and white geraniums, and you've got an instant centerpiece for a Fourth of July picnic. Tie a white, orange, and green bow (in honor of the Irish flag) to the handle of a wicker basket and use it to hold napkins for your Saint Patrick's Day party.

It pays to invest in quality ribbon that you can use over and over again. Look for various widths, and pick up whole reels of silk and French-wired ribbon—the kind with thin wires hemmed along the edges —when they go on sale at craft stores.

Artificial fruits and vegetables. Sometimes nothing beats the real thing, but a stash of wooden, wax, papier-mâché, or ceramic produce can be a useful addition to a decorating stockpile. For one thing, it never goes bad. So when you've invited guests for a spur-of-the-moment Thanksgiving toast before you go on to dinner at your neighbor's house, you can pull together an instant basket of plenty for the coffee table. Toss shiny red papier-mâché apples and some pine sprigs into a white bowl and it looks Christmassy. Omit the pine sprigs and add a blue ribbon, and the

and blue for the Fourth of July; or mums in autumnal tones of orange, gold, and copper for Halloween and Thanksgiving.

Your collection. Whether your taste is whimsical or down-home casual, a collection is a useful decorating tool. You might gather vases, trays, or even accent lamps with designs for every occasion: plain ones

Once you have a collection of baskets, pots, or wreaths, a few trimmings are all you'll need to create holiday-specific decorations.

look says Fourth of July. Or entwine red and white ribbons around the bowl for Valentine's Day. Import stores offer a fine selection of artificial fruit made of wood, ceramic, or papier-mâché.

Strings of lights. The little white ones that gleam from outdoor trees at Christmastime are also useful for everything from casting a romantic glow on a Valentine's Day dinner for two to lighting up a nighttime Labor Day clambake, and they're well worth stocking up on at after-Christmas sales. But for sheer fun, treat yourself to a few strands in festive shapes and colors. Your grapevine wreath could then wear tiny ghost lights for Halloween, red and white heart lights for Valentine's Day, or chili peppers for Cinco de Mayo.

Flowers. An assortment of dried flowers can produce instant holiday decor. Use the kind that hold their colors well—roses, bachelor's buttons, statice—and mix and match them to suit the occasion. Or spruce up soft, faded shades with colored ribbon. And don't overlook fresh flowers. Put red tulips in a white vase for Valentine's Day; anemones in vibrant shades of red, white,

covered with shamrocks or little hearts, or shaped ones resembling Christmas trees, Easter eggs, or pilgrim hats.

Once you have assembled even a few decorating elements, the possibilities are nearly endless. And once you have developed the habit of seeing treasures everywhere you look, you'll be able to produce holiday atmosphere in less time than it takes to whip up dessert.

A Tree for Every Holiday

Who says that decorated trees are only for Christmas? Designate a tree in your garden or a large potted plant in your house as the holiday tree, and trim it up with plastic eggs for Easter, miniature pumpkins for Halloween, plastic champagne flutes for New Year's, or paper hearts for Valentine's Day.

GIVING the PERFECT Gift

—✳—

1 Decide ahead of time whom you want to give presents to this holiday season and how much you want to spend. **2** Enter your gift list in your pocket notebook and keep it with you to **spark ideas** when you're in a store. **3** Do your shopping throughout the year in stores and mail-order **catalogs.** Look for seasonal sales. **4** When you are really under the gun, shop late and schedule gift giving for **after** the holidays. **5** To avoid stress, **shun malls** and shop in neighborhood and small downtown stores. **6** Simplify the big family **gift exchange** by drawing names or by giving one gift to each family. **7** Instead of a material gift, consider giving a **gift of time**—offer your gardening expertise or give tennis lessons. **8** Let gift-giving **creativity** flow for Valentine's Day, birthdays, Easter, and Mother's and Father's Days. **9** Make a gift much more special by presenting it in a clever way, such as via a **scavenger** hunt. **10** Keep a **stash** of gifts and wrappings on hand so you'll be prepared when you need a last-minute present for any occasion. ●

GIVING MADE SIMPLE

FINDING AND GIVING
GIFTS FROM THE HEART

——❋——

Few of us would dispute that the act of giving ranks among the greatest joys of Christmas or any other season. For some, giving gifts is almost a way of life. We all know people who never fail to produce just the right present for each recipient, no matter what the occasion. Then there are those of us who fret over every detail: Are our Kwanzaa gifts simple and meaningful enough? Should we give the kids just a little gelt and only on the first night of Hanukkah? And as for Christmas, how much is too much when it comes to giving presents to our spouses, children, friends, coworkers, and a growing family of nieces, nephews, and in-laws?

Only you can decide where to draw the line. But with careful planning, you can take the stress out of holiday shopping—and all the wrapping and mailing involved—and focus your energy instead on the joy of giving.

MAKING A LIST

———— ✳ ————

D OES THE VERY IDEA OF HOLIDAY GIFT SHOPPING MAKE YOU WANT TO RUN
AND HIDE? IT DOES FOR MANY PEOPLE, AND THE REASONS VARY GREATLY.
SOME ABHOR THE CROWDS THAT THRONG EVERY STREET AND MALL.

Others feel pressured to give more presents than they'd like or to spend more money than they can afford. Yet others feel that society places too much emphasis on gifts and too little on the spiritual aspects of the holidays. Then there are those who love everything about the gift-giving ritual and wouldn't change a thing—they just wish they had more time to devote to it.

There is no right or wrong approach to gift giving. If you and the members of your extended family find untold joy in searching out wondrous treasures for each

The Christmas wishes *of a young child can be easy to satisfy, but time and cost can mount if the list is long. Try focusing on one major gift rather than several smaller ones.*

other, or if you look forward all year long to the excitement provoked by those be-ribboned mounds on Christmas morning, go for it. If you can spare the time, it will be a labor of love. However, if you feel that gift giving has gotten out of hand, trim back in whatever way you see fit, regardless of whether you're motivated by a tight budget or the desire to focus on spiritual gifts rather than material ones.

THE PLAN

No matter how long or how short your gift list, your life will be much easier if you have a plan. Decide whom you want to give presents to this year and roughly what you want to spend overall, and re-solve to stay within the budget you have

established. You might even want to rule out the use of credit cards for your gift purchases; by paying for every present as you buy it, you can steer clear of one of the most common sources of postholiday stress—the bills that arrive in January.

Enter the gift list in your small pocket notebook (see page 22), giving each person a page or two. If you have specific ideas for presents, jot them down along with any other data that will be useful as you roam the stores—clothing sizes, favorite colors, hobbies, and interests (even if you know these particulars, they tend to slip your mind just when you need them the most). While you're at it, list the presents you've already given each person over the past year or two to avoid giving the same thing twice. Also include the presents that you've received from them in years past, as these gifts will give you insight into the personal tastes of their respective givers.

Holiday Gift File

Throughout the year, keep a file or large envelope hidden in a dresser drawer (out of sight of prying eyes) or at your office. Whenever you find something in a catalog, newspaper, or flier that might make a suitable gift, store the information in your file. When you find time, open the file and order the gifts, or schedule a shopping blitz.

Or if you're out running Saturday errands with your daughter and she sees the bicycle of her dreams in a store window, wait till she's distracted with another toy and write down the details. When you get home, call the store and ask them to hold the bike—

If you rule out the use of credit cards for gift purchases, you'll avoid one of the most common sources of holiday stress—the bills that follow.

Acquire the habit of keeping your notebook within reach and your ears open. That way, when you're speaking to your mother on the phone and she says, "I just heard the most fascinating interview with the author of a bird-watching book"— and you've noted that bird-watching is your new brother-in-law's passion—you can write the book title beside his name. When you get a chance, comb your notebook for any book titles you've written down and order them all at once from your local bookstore or over the Internet.

and while you're at it, have the folks at the store put it together. Santa has more than enough to do on Christmas Eve.

HIDDEN TREASURES
Bear in mind that gifts often lurk in the least likely places. That old wooden trunk in front of the thrift store might be just the thing for your sister, who, as you've jotted down in your notebook, has recently enrolled in a furniture-painting class. A poster announcing a Louis Malle film festival might remind you that your nephew

EASY GIFTS

---✳---

IF YOU'RE HAVING TROUBLE THINKING OF a gift for someone, consider making a present from a collection of smaller items. A quick trip to a hobby shop or another store that sells the individual components is all the shopping you need to do.

▲ **A fragrant bundle** *of Yule "logs," tied with dried herbs, scents the house when burned.*

◀ **A fun bowl** *filled with dog treats will keep your beloved family pooch occupied during the Christmas gift exchange.*

▲ **A basket** *of stationery, rubber stamps, pens, and pressed flowers is perfect for anyone who loves to send notes and cards.*

▲ **Fill a planter** *with packets of seeds, bulbs, and tools for a gardener.*

is majoring in French and that he'd probably love a book of passes to the local theater specializing in foreign films. Keep your list with you and your eyes peeled even after the holidays have passed. When you see something you know Uncle Willie or your sister Sarah would love, buy it and tuck it away. Catalogs drift through the mail slot all year; you don't have to wait for the ones marked "Christmas." Call in early orders for fancy smoked meats, cheeses, savory sauces, or fruits and nuts for your out-of-town relatives, and specify the shipping date. Or make things even easier: If you know the recipient is an enthusiastic cook, for instance, simply dial up a mail-order cookware supplier and purchase a gift certificate. Be creative and diligent, and you may have most of your Christmas shopping done by September.

CHRISTMAS POSTPONED

If you're really feeling under the gun this year, your best course may be simple procrastination. You don't *have* to exchange Christmas gifts on December 24 or 25. Instead, schedule your festivities for January 6—Christmas Eve on the Orthodox calendar (on other Christian calendars, it's known as the Feast of the Epiphany, Twelfth Night, and El Día de los Reyes). Whatever you choose to call it, the day the Three Wise Men arrived at the manger bearing their gifts of gold, frankincense, and myrrh is probably a more appropriate day to exchange presents anyway.

It can also be fun to spread the joy by staggering your gift giving over the entire 12 days after Christmas—December 26

to January 6. Not only does it let you delay at least some of your shopping if you want to—thereby taking advantage of the post-holiday sales—but it also avoids the after-Christmas letdown that strikes so many people on the 26th. This is *not* to suggest that Santa change the day of his deliveries

You don't have to exchange gifts on December 24 or 25—spreading out the ritual can greatly simplify your life during the holidays.

to those who expect him. For young children, tradition is vital. What you do is not nearly as important as the fact that you do it every year, without fail. As kids get into their teenage years, however, it's another matter, and spreading gift-exchange rituals among friends and family can greatly simplify holiday life for grown-ups.

Everything Takes Longer

At the height of the holidays, more people are filling stores and parking lots, more people are making appointments for haircuts, and more people are booking flights and reserving restaurant tables. Wherever your holiday duties take you, allow at least one-third more time to travel, shop, and dine.

Avoid eleventh-hour frustration by buying
gifts that come preassembled.

If you're Jewish, gift giving is inherently simpler because Hanukkah presents are typically given only to children, and the traditional gift is a small amount of gelt, or money—no shopping required. But if your child is expecting eight lavish presents—one on each night of Hanukkah—and if nightly gift giving is a family tradition, there are still simpler ways to go. One is to give a series of small gifts that add up to something bigger, such as books in a series or dolls or toy cars for a collection. Another idea is to give one major present on the first night and more modest gifts, such as hollow dreidels filled with candy or small mesh bags of chocolate coins, on subsequent nights. Or you could reserve each successive night for gifts from different members of the family. For example, on the first night you could dole out the gifts from you and your spouse; on the

second and third nights, gifts from each set of grandparents; on the fourth night, gifts from one aunt and uncle; and so on.

In mixed marriages, kids may expect —and receive—presents for both Hanukkah and Christmas. One way to make this less taxing, and less of a contest between the traditions, is to pick a time to exchange "holiday" gifts among your immediate family. The holidays themselves could be reserved for opening presents from Jewish and Christian relatives, respectively, or just reflecting on the meaning of the day. If Hanukkah and Christmas overlap that year, so much the better.

DON'T GET MALLED

No matter what tradition you follow, by far the surest way to take the stress out of holiday shopping is simply to avoid the malls. Even at the slowest seasons of the year they can be crowded, noisy, and confusing. At holiday time, just finding parking can take the better part of a morning.

If you hate to fight crowds but you still like getting out during the holiday season, shop at smaller downtown stores and neighborhood shops as an alternative

Fans of catalog and Internet shopping swear they've found the cure for crowded malls and department stores at holiday time.

to malls. Your selections won't be so varied, but that alone can simplify life greatly. With fewer decisions to make, you can choose more quickly. There's no law saying that if your three-year-old wants a dump truck you have to scour every store in the mall, looking for one that might be shinier than the rest or hold two more pieces of cargo. Go to a good local toy store (in your own neighborhood or someone else's) and buy the first dump truck you think your child will like. A young child is easily pleased with almost any toy.

People who are fans of catalog and Internet shopping swear they've found the cure for crowded department stores—and those methods do have their advantages: You can buy almost anything you want, at any hour of the day or night, from the comfort and privacy of your own home.

Cruising catalogs is a low-tech solution for shoppers short on time, and the Internet has become a high-tech alternative. But don't assume that either method will necessarily eliminate all your stress.

Many a long-distance shopper has been disappointed to find that what arrived from a catalog or an online resource was smaller or less deluxe than what its photograph promised. If you choose a gift from a catalog or over the Web and have it sent sight unseen, you'll never know what actually arrived, and the recipient of an inferior product will probably be too polite to tell you. The solution: The first year you deal with an untried supplier, order far in advance and have your purchase shipped directly to you. That way you can check it out before you give it, thus avoiding disappointment and embarrassment.

GIVING THE CATALOG

One of the best ways to find catalog merchandise you know you can trust is to order from a company whose retail stores are already familiar to you. If you've been pleased with the quality and service you've

Escaping Crowds

If you must hit the malls and you can't go on weekdays when they're less crowded, you can usually count on fewer crowds during the dinner hour. Another good time to shop is as soon as the stores open on Saturday or Sunday. The day *before* Thanksgiving and late afternoon on Christmas Eve are also surprisingly crowd-free times.

received in person at stores like Williams-Sonoma, Smith & Hawken, Eddie Bauer, Crate & Barrel, or Pottery Barn, you can order with confidence from their catalogs. An added advantage is the fact that if any of your recipients decide to exchange their presents, they can simply take them to the store closest to where they live.

Catalogs themselves can be great gifts. The garden world abounds in small mail-order nurseries whose catalogs are gold mines of plant lore and design inspiration. If there's a gardener or would-be gardener on your list, order a few reliable catalogs and give them along with a gift certificate for each catalog. You'll find small and large mail-order nurseries listed in garden magazines, in garden articles in interior design magazines, and on the Internet.

Shopping in neighborhood *stores is often much easier than fighting downtown traffic. You'll also find more one-of-a-kind gifts than the department stores offer.*

There is almost nothing you cannot buy through a mail-order catalog, but unless it's your only option, you should avoid gifts the recipient would want to try on or try out—ice skates, for instance, or a state-of-the-art tennis racket. It's better to buy that sort of thing locally so that if it doesn't work out, the recipient can take it back and choose its replacement carefully.

ONE-STOP SHOPPING

Think beyond the obvious choices of malls and department stores, and you can come up with novel gifts—you might even get all your shopping done (gift wrapping and tags included) in one place. For instance:

Hardware stores. How many people do you know who wouldn't like to have a really good flashlight or a cordless electric screwdriver? Even people who have them can always use another. Buy one for everybody. Better yet, put together some tool kits—powered screwdrivers and flashlights included—for all the new home owners or college grads on your list. Buy sets of child-size garden tools for all the kids; and pick out a hammer, measuring tape, and some picture hooks for your poster-collecting niece who just moved to a new apartment.

These days most hardware stores sell everything from flower pots to toys and kitchen gadgets, so without stretching your imagination very far you might be able to zip through your list in less than an hour.

Bookstores. Even if there are people on your list who don't like to read, you could probably do all your holiday shopping in a local bookstore. If you've found a cookbook you can't get along without, buy one for everybody. For the collector on your list, look for books, calendars, or note cards featuring relevant subject matter: Amish quilts, Italian pottery, or Barbie dolls. If you don't have the slightest clue about someone's hobbies or interests, look for blank journals and scrapbooks, address books, even cartoon collections.

Or, because there's a little bit of child in all of us at Christmastime, buy everyone a classic children's book—*Winnie-the-Pooh, The Secret Garden, Alice's Adventures in Wonderland, Little Women,* or *Charlotte's Web* (while you're at it, tuck in a couple of other E. B. White masterpieces, *Stuart Little* and *The Trumpet of the Swan*).

FOR BODY AND SOUL

Toy stores. Speaking of the child in everyone, try giving the grown-ups in your life replicas of antique windup toys. Look for ducks riding bicycles, seals spinning balls on their snouts, elephants dancing on

One Size Fits All

For the ultimate in simplicity, give the same gift to all the adults on your list. Food baskets fit easily into this category. Other likely choices are picture frames, photo albums, pocket or disposable cameras, cordless electric screwdrivers, narcissi or other potted flowers, books of movie passes, comprehensive cookbooks, wine, or cookware.

storage containers in the most grown-up office, kitchen, or bathroom in town. If your list includes stuffed-animal collectors or devotees of particular kinds of critters— or simply someone with a well-developed sense of the whimsical—a toy store can be a dream come true. Get the whale lover

Consider buying everyone on your list a classic children's book: There's a little bit of child in all of us during the Christmas season.

drums, or Ferris wheels whirling above tin midways. They're easy to find, many are priced low enough for the tightest office-Secret-Santa budget, and they're all but guaranteed to delight even the most strait-laced member of your board of directors. Other sure bets for producing adult merriment are Hula Hoop and Slinky toys, yo-yos, and bubble pipes.

Toy stores often sell boxes and tins that not only make clever (and fast) wrappings but are also attractive enough to serve as

a pod of plastic humpbacks, blues, minkes, and orcas to line up along the bathroom shelf. You'll also find animal-themed jigsaw puzzles, playing cards, picture books, posters, board games, and T-shirts—and often an excellent selection of tree ornaments in a variety of animal shapes.

Gourmet food shops. Many places that specialize in prepared take-out meals are also sources of excellent jams and jellies, chutneys, salsas, and dessert sauces, as well as wines and microbrews. Often you'll also

Hallowed Hauls

For some terrific food gifts, try abbeys and monasteries. Many of them throughout Canada, the United States, and Europe produce some of the best cheeses, jams, honeys, breads, and cakes you'll find. They may also sell religious crafts. Most will provide mail-order service, but if you find one close to your home, a visit makes a delightful trip.

find table linens, cooking gadgets, cookbooks, and recipe files. Give a budding teenage chef a few good culinary tools, a cookbook, and some ingredients for one of the recipes inside. Buy a Little Leaguer a few bags of pasta in the shapes of bats, balls, and gloves, along with a favorite jar

> **If you give potted bulbs at Christmas, they'll bloom in late January to mid-February—a perfect time for a jolt of cheering color.**

of sauce. Chances are you'll be able to find novelty pastas for other people on your gift list—these days they come in shapes ranging from sports equipment to musical instruments and angels.

Nurseries and garden shops. These are obvious stops when you're out to please the gardeners in your life. But here treasures await even those who have never so much

as put hand to shovel. There is probably no adult in the world who wouldn't be happy to have a big colorful amaryllis or pot of forced paperwhite narcissi. For instant gratification, buy plants that are already potted and in full bloom. But you can save money and easily pot up a few bulbs yourself in attractive containers—or have the store do it for you. If you give potted bulbs at Christmas, they'll bloom in late January to mid-February—just when many of us could do with a jolt of cheering color. For that bonsai enthusiast, you might pick up a special pair of pruning shears. For someone who likes to cook, buy pots of fresh herbs, or a beautiful cast-stone or pottery urn (without a drainage hole) to use as a wine cooler.

Like hardware and houseware stores, garden shops and nurseries have branched out far beyond their original niches. Many of them sell vases, candleholders, baskets—even dishes, clothes, and furniture for indoors and out. The pickings will be slimmer for kids than for adults, but chances are you'll find a child-size chair or a pair of Wellies just like Christopher Robin's. And you'll be able to find a selection of kids' gardening books, small watering cans and trowels, and easy-to-grow plants that could launch a future master gardener.

BEYOND PLANTS

Supermarkets. The big ones sell many of the same things you'd find in hardware stores, gourmet food shops, and nurseries. They also have two major advantages over just about any other store you can think of: (1) you have to go there anyway, often two to three times a week, and (2) most of them are open at least until the early evening hours of Christmas Eve, and some are open 24 hours a day. Even the world's worst procrastinator can dive in at the last minute and come up with more than a few winning presents. Aside from fancy foods, most supermarkets also sell house-plants, flowers, basic carpentry and gardening tools, kitchen gear, photo albums, and cameras (disposable and otherwise). In some locales, supermarkets offer a large selection of wines, liqueurs, and spirits. You'll even find audiocassettes, videocassettes, and books. The shelves may not be packed with great literature, but there are often broad selections of mysteries and popular fiction, and frequently a range of gardening, cooking, and how-to titles.

And when you're *really* pressed for time, there's always a magazine subscription. Even 24-hour convenience stores sell magazines. Wrap the current issue with a card saying more will follow.

Still stumped for a gift? See page 138 for a comprehensive list of further suggestions, organized by category of recipient.

TOO MANY TO BUY FOR

Even people who have holiday shopping down to a science can feel overwhelmed when new in-laws and new babies send the gift list soaring. But there are ways to bring more fun to the annual gathering while simplifying life for all concerned. One tried-and-true method is the names-in-a-hat technique: Everyone draws a name and buys a gift only for that person. You can choose a theme to save everyone the agony of figuring out what to buy, or you can level the financial playing field by setting a price limit. You can even suggest that everyone spend on their chosen recipient

Window-shopping *can be a good way to come up with gift ideas. Take a partner or friend for a holiday excursion and browse, letting your imagination flow.*

about what they'd pay if they bought gifts for all. To keep kids from feeling cheated out of the mound of presents every child hopes for, have every adult buy presents for the children under 12.

Or try this alternative: Each family member brings a gift to the gathering without knowing who will receive it. Then everyone draws a number. Whoever draws number one selects any package under the tree and opens it. Number two then has the choice of opening an unknown present from under the tree or claiming number one's gift. Numbers three, four, and so on can choose any gift already opened or unwrap a new present. Whenever someone loses a gift, he or she can then take someone else's gift or unwrap a new present. The only stipulation is that a single gift may exchange hands no more than three times.

If games aren't your style, start a custom of giving one gift to each family rather than selecting something for each individual. Give your sister, her husband, and their kids a family-size toboggan. Surprise your parents with a tandem bike. Treat your brother's family to a croquet set. You get to bestow a more lavish gift for the same money you'd spend on several smaller gifts, and you spend far less time shopping.

Another idea is to suggest that everyone give a gift of family history. This is an especially thoughtful approach for families whose older members are on limited incomes. Suggest that they write out time-tested family recipes or record the stories of their lives and those of their parents. It's also a lot of fun for children, who can render the family's history as a series of crayon drawings, paintings, or written narratives.

WRAPPING IT UP

For the ultimate in simplicity, buy your gifts in stores that will wrap and ship them for you. Any extra charge will be more than made up for by the time and energy you save—and in some cases the wrapping fee benefits local charities. But if you're a person who looks forward to adorning your own holiday gifts, play the game to the hilt. Set aside time just for wrapping. Send the kids to their grandparents' or have your spouse take them iceskating. Then gather your supplies, clear a big table to work on, make yourself a cup of hot apple cider, pop your favorite Christmas music into the CD player, and go to it. Aside from giving you a chance to indulge in a favorite holiday ritual, designating a day for wrapping has a whopping advantage over the wrap-it-as-you-buy-it approach: It forces you to get all your shopping done early. It's also easier to pull out all the equipment—tape, scissors, ribbon, paper, cards—just once during the season.

A Christmas stocking *is the perfect wrapping for a selection of colorful socks.*

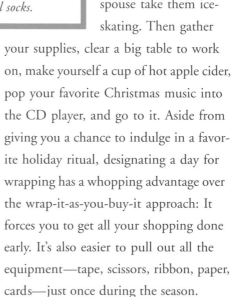

GIFT WRAP IN A SNAP

❋

WRAPPING GIFTS CREATIVELY doesn't have to take up a lot of your time. With a little imagination—and a few easy-to-find accessories—you can make even the most humdrum present stand out under the tree. Here are a few handy ideas.

▲ **A scarf** *tied with decorative accents is an attractive alternative to gift paper.*

▼ **A folding beverage carton** *is ideal for small gifts. Glue wrapping paper to its sides or spray-paint it in a holiday color.*

▲ **Patterned or foil-covered** *bags make wrapping easy: Fold the top, punch holes, and thread with ribbon to prevent peeking.*

▲ **Pack gifts with color** *by gluing on cutouts from magazines and tying on bright ribbon.*

NO WAITING

YOU NEED TO SEND PACKAGES all over the country but you've seen the lines at the post office and the private shipping companies—and you can't face the wait. What do you do? Have someone else pack and ship the presents for you.

 Simple Take your wrapped presents to a packaging store, which will pack your gifts and ship them. Some of these places will even come to your house or business to pick up your packages.

Simpler Purchase your gifts at a major department store and have the store ship them for you. Most stores will also wrap the gifts for you and include a personalized card with each package.

Simplest Order your gifts from a catalog or the Internet and have them shipped directly to your recipient. If you say it's a gift, the company will send the bill to you and the wrapped package to your recipient.

The wrapping can be as elaborate or as simple as you choose to make it. But some of the most impressive results can be the easiest to achieve. It takes only seconds to gather a piece of fabric around a package and tie it with a cord or ribbon and perhaps tuck in a small sprig of holly or pine. Depending on whether you use silk cord on velvet or burlap tied with brightly colored twine, the effect can be the height of elegance or rustic enough to win cheers from your five-year-old cowboy.

SHIPPING

If the treasures that you've shopped for and wrapped so lovingly will be traveling out of town without you, by far the simplest, and safest, thing to do is take them to a store that will pack and ship them. (Look under "Shipping" in the Yellow Pages.) If you decide to handle the project yourself, however, be sure to use sturdy outer boxes

and to pad the inner containers well (even if your gifts aren't fragile ones) with bubble wrap, Styrofoam "peanuts" or real popcorn

When shipping gifts, avoid frustration by allowing extra time and by assuming it will cost more than you expect.

(air-popped with no salt or butter), or shredded or wadded paper. Use plain paper rather than newspaper—newsprint rubs off onto anything it touches.

Postal and shipping rates change frequently, as do your carrier options. Even packing guidelines can vary from one year to the next. Check with your post office or a private carrier for the latest details, but avoid frustration by allowing more time than you think you need, and by assuming it will cost more than you expect.

GIFTS WITH A DIFFERENCE

———— ✳ ————

SOME OF THE BEST HOLIDAY GIFTS—AND THE EASIEST TO SHOP FOR—DON'T
COME IN PACKAGES. IF YOU WANT TO LESSEN THE EMPHASIS ON MATERIALISM
OR JUST FIND A WELCOME GIFT, THERE ARE MANY SIMPLE OPTIONS.

First, consider a gift of time. In today's busy world, time freely given is a treasured commodity. Think about what you do or know best and make up a gift certificate for your services. Give someone tennis, golf, or kayaking lessons; share your expertise in gardening, carpentry, or interior design—or give a certificate for professional lessons or services. Cater a dinner for your friends and their chosen guests, or conduct a walking tour of your town.

Consider giving a single parent or a busy working couple time to themselves. If you're not inclined to watch their kids for a night or a weekend, hire a sitter; or give them a commercial maid service that will clean the house from top to bottom while they take the kids out for a day of fun.

THE ADVENTURE GIFT

A close cousin to the gift of time is the Dutch-treat adventure, which makes a great alternative to material gifts for many people on your list—your best pal at work, longtime friends, and all those relatives who insist that they don't need another gift because they already have more stuff than they know what to do with. A shared

Grandparents, aunts, and uncles will treasure
gifts that children make themselves.

Handmade Holidays

You'll find many inexpensive yet beautifully crafted handmade gifts when you browse craft fairs, senior centers, and holiday bazaars sponsored by neighborhood schools, churches, and community centers. Handmade items make excellent gifts for people who appreciate the time and talent that go into producing each unique creation.

adventure not only saves shopping time and puts off spending till after you've dealt with the Christmas bills, but it also gives you a chance to enjoy the company of the people you care about, free of the distractions of holiday revelry. Suggest to your sister that instead of exchanging gifts this year, the two of you take a weekend jaunt to the lake where you spent summers as children. Plan a day trip with friends to a nearby theater festival, or have Sunday brunch at a restaurant and spend the afternoon cruising nearby antique shops.

KID-MADE GIFTS

Holidays are an opportunity to encourage your child's own generosity. Even before they turn two or three, most children have grasped the concept of giving things to the special people in their lives. They may not be old enough for elaborate projects, but if you roll out some cookie dough, they're perfectly capable of pressing in the cookie

cutters. The results won't look like they came from the pastry kitchen at the Ritz, but the pride in your children's eyes when they present Grandma with the sugar cookies they made themselves will more than compensate for a few rough edges.

For kids six or seven on up, beeswax candles are great gifts to make. They're elegant enough to please the most sophisticated grown-up decorator, and the basic process couldn't be simpler: You simply roll a sheet of wax around a length of wick and, presto, you have a candle. You can find wax, wicks, and detailed instructions in almost any craft store.

Give your children's budding talents a boost by keeping a stash of art supplies and collage makings. It's the perfect way to use all those odd bits of ribbon, yarn, colorful papers and foils—even postcards—that come your way. Some of your kids' artistic efforts might become the covers of homemade coupon books, with tickets that are redeemable for their snow-shoveling, leaf-raking, or car-washing services.

Just as you nurture their natural generosity, encourage your kids' feelings of gratitude. A six-year-old's drawing made with the markers Uncle John gave her would make a treasured thank-you note. So would a message scrawled in her unique alphabet. Instill the thank-you-note habit early. And set a precedent of writing them by hand, even if it's just a sentence or two. It takes only a few minutes, and it's the most gracious way to say thank you. (During the excitement of present opening, have your notebook handy so you can keep track of who gave what to which child; this list will prove invaluable when the time comes to get your children to write their thank-yous.)

If you or the kids are unable to make something yourselves, buying the handiwork of local artists and craftspeople is

cares as much about the cause as you do). For an environmentalist or animal lover of any age, you can "adopt" a manatee in Florida, a gray whale off the California coast, or a humpback off Cape Cod. The adoptive "parent" receives a certificate of

Give kids' budding talents a boost by keeping a stash of art supplies: ribbon, yarn, colorful papers and foils—even postcards.

a wonderful alternative. You can buy your gifts (and your cards) at holiday bazaars that benefit good causes ranging from UNICEF to your local botanical garden.

A GOOD CAUSE

In some towns, retailers and distributors donate merchandise to a temporary holiday store, with all the proceeds going to charities that help children. Your purchases may not be handcrafted, but they'll benefit more than just their recipients. You can also give your friends memberships in nonprofit groups (just be sure the recipient

adoption, a photograph or two of the animal, a complete history and family profile, and periodic updates on his or her health and whereabouts. The adoption package, combined with a stuffed whale or manatee, makes a great gift for a child.

An alternative is simple, unalloyed altruism: Make a donation in the recipient's name to his or her favorite charity, which will send an acknowledgment card.

Harness your kids' *enthusiasm for baking: Have them make and decorate holiday cookies to give to neighbors and friends.*

GIFTS FOR ALL SEASONS

———— ✳ ————

MANY PEOPLE WHO FIND GIFT GIVING STRESSFUL AT YEAR'S END LOVE IT IN OTHER SEASONS, WHEN THE COMPETITION FOR MERCHANDISE, WRAPPING PAPER, AND PARKING SPACES IS MUCH LESS INTENSE.

Even those people who seem to thrive during the bustle of December shopping may gain much greater satisfaction from finding or making the perfect token of their affections for Valentine's Day, Easter, Mother's Day, or Father's Day—or for no particular occasion at all.

VALENTINE'S DAY

Gifts of love can take many forms other than the standard chocolate and cut flowers. For instance, if the object of your affections is a gardener, accompany the usual

Gathering a *Mother's Day bouquet can be a wonderful way for the two of you to share the day. Press the blossoms later for a memento.*

dozen red roses with a bare-root or potted rosebush that will bloom year after year. Choose from roses with apt names such as 'Angel Face,' 'Sheer Bliss,' or 'Love,' 'Honor,' and 'Cherish'—varieties that also happen to be highly rated for flower production, cold hardiness, and disease resistance. You can order bare-root roses by mail or find them at garden centers.

Or go beyond roses and give flowers or plants that appear in the works of a favorite author. If your loved one is a fan of detective mysteries, give a collection of herbs used by Ellis Peters's monk-detective, Brother Cadfael. (Many are available in herb shops and nurseries year-round, and they'll thrive on a sunny windowsill until it's time to plant them in the garden.) Shakespeare's sonnets and plays are also full of references to plants. Give seed packets of columbine, daisies, or carnations (known to the Bard as gillyflowers), and include a flower press to ensure that the memory of your gift lasts.

If plants and flowers don't interest you, there are other novel and simple ways to demonstrate your love on Valentine's Day. For example, try a pared-down version of Richard Wagner's famous gift to his beloved Cosima. He quietly assembled an orchestra string section on the stairway of their house, and when Cosima woke in her bedroom on that Christmas morning, she heard for the first time the opening strains of the overture to *Siegfried Idyll,* named for their infant son. You probably can't pull that off, but you can call your local musicians' union and ask them to send over a trio of string players, or even a solo guitarist, to perform a surprise serenade. (You could even support budding artists by hiring music students from a nearby college.) Follow up with a romantic dinner for two, dropped off by a caterer or a restaurant-delivery service.

EASTER

If you'd like to give a child an Easter basket —or make one as a host or hostess gift— there are easy ways to celebrate spring and Christ's rebirth without contributing to tooth decay. You can fill a child's basket with a number of stuffed animals (chicks, bunnies, and lambs are traditional), plastic eggs filled with small toys or marbles, or books about Easter or springtime. A very young child would appreciate a picture book featuring bunnies and chicks.

A beautifully simple Easter gift for an adult could be a pot of tulips, crocuses, or freesias tucked into a basket with a pastel-colored bow tied to the handle. You could also give a basket brimming with potted herbs or bulbs of summer-blooming flowers. With a little more effort, you can create a "live" Easter basket with real grass: Three weeks before Easter, fill a small, flat pot (make sure it has drainage holes) with potting soil and sprinkle grass seed over it. Water it daily and leave it in the sun or on a sunny windowsill. When the

RED ROSES ARE ALWAYS RIGHT FOR YOUR SWEETHEART, BUT FOR CHERISHED FRIENDS ALSO CONSIDER THESE SIMPLE GIFTS.

Rose tree

A "tree" made of dried roses is ideal for a friend who lives in a city apartment but longs for a garden. The fragrant rose ball, set in a pot as if it were a live tree rose, is evocative of a formal garden in bloom.

Antique cards

Antique-reproduction prints featuring Cupids and flowers make touching Valentine cards for friends and family members who are far away but close to your heart. You can often find these in stationery stores.

Potpourri

Nearly everyone will appreciate a bowl of potpourri to spice up a living room or bedroom. Purchase a box imprinted with sentimental images and fill it with a potpourri made of fragrant dried flowers.

Heart-shaped boxes

Boxes formed in the shape of hearts can spruce up any Valentine gift. Into one, place a reservation notice for an evening at a romantic bed-and-breakfast for you and your sweetheart; fill another with candy hearts for a child. For the simplest Valentine of all, just insert a message saying "I love you."

Online Photo Album

If your parents live far away and miss seeing their grandchildren, consider giving them an online photo album. It's easier than you think: Have your photos scanned at a copy shop, or have film processed onto a CD-ROM. Then just attach the digitized photos to an e-mail message. You can send weekly or monthly updates as the kids grow up.

grass has grown a few inches, tuck the pot inside a basket and nestle brightly colored Easter eggs in the grass.

MOM AND DAD

Finding gifts for Mother's Day or Father's Day can be challenging, especially if your parents insist—as many do—that they don't want you to buy them anything; they have enough *things* already. If your parents are music lovers, you could give them a concert much like the one you arranged for a valentine—just shift the mood from romantic to sentimental.

You also might give them time with you. Spend the afternoon playing golf with your father, then go on to drinks and dinner. Take your mother to dinner and a play you know she's been wanting to see. A prepaid phone card makes a thoughtful gift for a parent who lives far away; so does a year's worth of Internet service if they'd like to keep in touch by e-mail. Or give

Mom or Dad a class in something that you know they've been wanting to try—or get back into. Give them a gift certificate for a pottery class, a mushroom-identification hike, or tap-dancing lessons. Order them a subscription to a magazine—or several—that you know they'd love but aren't likely to order for themselves.

Even the simplest gift becomes more special when you deliver it in a clever way. For the young at heart, try having a scavenger hunt. Hide the gift, then wrap a series of clues in packages and scatter them throughout the house, even outside if the weather cooperates. In the simplest form of the game, the clues are directions written on slips of paper. For instance, when your father arrives at your house for his Father's Day dinner, he finds a box at the front door and opens it to see a note saying "Look behind the lamp in the living room." There, he finds another box whose contents might say "Look in the bathtub." And so on until he finds the treasure.

A prepaid phone card makes a thoughtful gift for a parent who lives far away; so does a year's worth of Internet service.

But with minimal extra effort, you can add more intrigue. Say, for instance, you have decided as a Mother's Day treat to take your mother to England for a tour of her favorite gardens. Along with the note in each box, you can include a more tangible clue. You might put a flower in the first box; a miniature shovel in the second; a photograph of an English garden in the third; continue with a book on famous gardens and a map of England that you've highlighted in the next two boxes; and finally, tucked into a suitcase, her plane ticket and the tour brochure.

A GIFT STASH

Whatever the season, one of the most useful social assets—and life simplifiers—that a person can have is a stash of presents laid by, just in case. Assign a cupboard or trunk for the purpose. Then have fun stocking it with bottles of wine, jars of preserves and chutneys, boxes of golf balls, and bags of potpourri. Acquire the habit of buying multiples. When you find a book you love, buy a few extras and tuck them away. Even if you don't have kids, include a few toys, children's books, and games. Include a supply of wrapping paper and ribbon in several colors, along with a dozen or more blank cards. Prewrap a few gifts, and attach a note to each so you'll remember what's inside.

Keeping a gift treasure chest is also a great way to avoid returning gifts or to find good homes for those things you would love to keep but can't. Should someone give you a second copy of *Joy of Cooking* or raspberry-filled candies that will rouse your allergies, simply add them to your stock and pass them on. (Just be sure to attach a note saying who gave you each gift so you don't give it back by mistake!)

When any holiday or birthday approaches, check your gift stash first. If you've stocked it wisely, and with the tastes of family and friends in mind, you won't need to go any farther. Your treasure chest can also save you from embarrassment at Christmastime if guests show up with a gift for you and you haven't bought anything for them. Perhaps best of all, it will let you avoid that last-minute scramble for a gift when friends invite you to the country for the weekend, your next-door neighbors throw an impromptu dinner party, or you remember as you leave for work that your brother-in-law's birthday party is scheduled for that very night.

Once you've learned to plan your gift-giving strategy, to shop during the year as inspiration strikes, and to keep an inventory of sure-to-please presents in reserve, you'll wonder why you ever thought that gift shopping was a chore.

Give Mom something that will grow on her.

HOLIDAY MEALS
MADE SIMPLE

------ ✳ ------

T HE MERE IDEA OF GIVING A SIT-DOWN DINNER PARTY HAS BEEN KNOWN TO
STRIKE TERROR IN THE HEARTS OF PEOPLE WHO THINK NOTHING OF SINGING
BEFORE A PACKED CONCERT HALL OR KAYAKING DOWN BOULDER-STREWN RAPIDS.

Even those who love showing off their culinary talents often find themselves stretched to the limit during the holidays. The good news is that you can produce a big family dinner that's as close to stress-free as nature and human personalities will allow.

PLANNING
Whether your family feast is commemorating Thanksgiving, Christmas, Kwanzaa, New Year's Day, Passover, or Easter, the logistics for a big dinner are essentially the same. As with all other aspects of the holidays, the first step in simplifying is to banish all thoughts of perfection (Norman Rockwell will not be painting your family at the table). The idea is to have an enjoyable and meaningful celebration with your family and friends, not to audition for a role on a home-entertaining TV show. Decide how much you want to do; then make a plan and carry it out.

You'll be able to please almost any guest
if you keep a well-stocked pantry.

The earlier you know what you're going to do, the easier it will be to make the arrangements. When you sat down in October to create a fall and winter game plan (see page 21), let's say you chose Thanksgiving as your pull-out-all-the-stops holiday. As soon as you know whom you're going to invite, call and ask everyone to save the date. (You can always add more people as you go along.)

Decide on a menu and jot down in your pocket notebook any ingredients you need, along with other supplies—edible and otherwise. Then you can buy everything (except perishables) at a discount warehouse, order items from a mail-order catalog, or pick them up as you do routine grocery shopping. That way, you'll keep last-minute chores to a minimum. Planning ahead also gives you time to experiment with new products before you incorporate them into your grand scheme. When you see wine on sale, try one bottle before buying a whole case. Take home a pie from that new bakery before you order six for Thanksgiving dinner.

If it's been a while since you used the good china, pull it out, note anything that needs to be replaced or supplemented, and add those items to your shopping list.

STOCKING UP

If you're able to plan even further ahead, take advantage of the summer's harvest: Gather fruits and vegetables from nearby produce stands. Make a big pot of vegetable soup, then freeze it in small containers (be sure to label and date them). Make herbal oils and vinegars that will

Durable Dishes

Paper and plastic plates are fine for cocktail-hour noshing or snacks. But if you're serving the traditional turkey dinner, steer clear—even the sturdiest disposable plates won't stand up to mashed potatoes and gravy. If your regular dishes won't suffice, borrow plates from a guest or buy an inexpensive set (plain white is always tasteful).

add instant sophistication to anything you serve. Put up jars of apricot-almond chutney, basil-spiked tomatoes, brandied peaches, or spicy apple butter. Preserving fruits and vegetables is a much simpler process than you think—check cookbooks or the cooking section of your local newspaper for recipes and inspiration.

On the other hand, if you don't relish all that cooking and canning, wait until the brisk autumn air stirs you to explore the countryside. Hop in your car and go. Get off the interstate and explore those winding roads that always look so enticing in magazine photographs. When you see roadside produce stands and farm markets, stop and buy jars of chutney and preserves, decorative bottles of flavorful oils and vinegars, and a selection of homemade cookies, breads, muffins, and other baked goods to freeze when you get home.

Whether the goodies come off the top of your stove or out of a shopping bag,

Keep staple foods *such as preserves and bottled sauces, cheeses, crackers, pastas, and frozen entrées on hand to feed extra guests or satisfy visitors with special dietary needs.*

you'll wind up with a supply of delicious food that will be ready to welcome visitors or feed your family at a moment's notice.

SELECTIVE EATERS

While you're stocking up, don't overlook the problem eaters who may be visiting. If you know in advance you'll be entertaining vegetarians, extra-picky kids, or people with allergies to everything from wheat to MSG, ask them (or their parents) which foods are OK. Don't feel obliged to build your menu around their tastes; just make sure that it includes something they'll like. When unexpected kids stay for dinner, you can't go wrong if you've stashed away some hot dogs or jars of peanut butter and jelly. Some good pasta and a jar of roasted red peppers in olive oil can quickly be transformed into a meal fit for any vegetarian.

As the days and evenings fill with choir practice and school pageants, with year-end work deadlines and drop-in guests, your freezer and your pantry become your two best friends. Never make just one casserole or pot of soup—make two or three instead. (Beware of multiplying a recipe, however—it can throw off seasoning ratios and cooking times. Unless the directions say the recipe can be doubled, you're usually better off making separate batches.) It takes only a little more time to make extra servings, and once you have an inventory of eggplant parmigiana and hearty vegetable-beef stew, you've got the basics for a casual dinner party or a quick bite before the family heads out to shop. Just warm up a loaf of crusty French bread (also from the freezer) and add a bagged, precut salad with bottled dressing.

When it comes time to shop for the things you couldn't—or didn't—buy far in advance, stick with stores where you know the layout. You've got better ways to spend your time than lost in the aisles of a strange supermarket, searching for the cheese counter. And remember, a good neighborhood market can save you a lot of time—and be more enjoyable to shop in than a big chain store, especially if you need only a few things.

There's another distinct advantage to a smaller market: The staff usually has more time to help you, and they can be

your recipe calls for, or to recommend a local microbrew that your visiting cousin from Milwaukee might like.

HOW MUCH TO MAKE?
When it comes to estimating quantities for your feast, remember that it always pays to cook more than you think you'll need. Figure on half a pound (225g) of

Stick with the stores you know. When you're rushed, you've got better ways to spend your time than lost in the aisles of a strange supermarket.

your best resource when you're under pressure. If you call from work and ask them to set aside a few bags of cranberries for you to pick up on your way home, chances are they'll be delighted to help you. Most likely, your grocer will also be happy to tell you what kind of onions will make the best substitutes for the out-of-season Vidalias

meat (without bone) per person, half to one cup (120–240ml) of each carbohydrate and vegetable, and one cup (240ml) of salad. For hors d'oeuvres, assume that each person will eat eight per hour. Regarding wine, if it's the only beverage you are serving to adults, allow half to one bottle per person. If that seems like a lot,

---

SIMPLE SOLUTIONS

PLEASING A GOURMET

IF YOUR RELATIVES' OR FRIENDS' TASTES tend toward four-star restaurants while you've barely mastered the art of hard-boiling eggs, don't worry about disappointing your guests. With a little ingenuity you can dazzle every would-be food critic.

Simple — Enlist the help of a friend. Perhaps your best friend is a chef, or your cousin just completed culinary school. Have him or her share a few tried-and-tested recipes with you and talk you through the steps.

Simpler — Barter your time. Ask that neighbor who's a gourmet cook to prepare your fancy side dishes and give you pointers on a simple entrée. In return, you'll do carpool duty or run household errands.

Simplest — Buy a meal from your local gourmet market or specialty take-out deli: Many of these feature traditional fare at holiday times. Devote your energy to creating the right atmosphere and serving the perfect wine.

---

remember that unopened bottles won't go bad and that it's cheaper to buy wine by the case than by the bottle.

When you're choosing wine, forget stereotypes about what color goes with what food. Buy what you like. If you don't have favorites, visit a wine store and ask for suggestions. For the ultimate in simplicity—and festivity—serve champagne. It goes with anything, nearly everyone likes it, and there's no better way to toast the health and happiness of your guests.

ALL THE TRIMMINGS

The ritual feast of roast meat, side dishes, and rich desserts is probably easier to simplify than any other aspect of holiday life. You don't even have to lift a finger if you don't want to. If your house is too small to contain your entire family or you just don't want to deal with the fuss of a major get-together, don't do it. Reserve space at

No Room at the Inn

When you're cooking a big holiday meal, you may run short of burners on the stove. Rather than fix some dishes early and reheat them, find some you can cook with the main course in the oven. Coat new potatoes, onions, carrots, parsnips, or other root vegetables with olive oil to roast in a shallow pan. Or, if space in the oven is tight, just set baking potatoes on the racks.

a restaurant—on your tab or Dutch treat. Maximize your options—and ease your mind—by making reservations early.

Even if you decide to serve dinner at home, you can virtually eliminate cooking. Most cities have at least a few restaurants,

---

Make dinner a joint effort: Assign each guest a dish—even furnish recipes if you're particular. Some guests can bring wine or flowers.

---

gourmet delis, or hotels that produce full —and delicious—holiday meals to go. All you have to do is warm the food and serve it on your own china. Or make dinner a joint effort: Assign a dish to each guest— even furnish the recipes if you're very particular. If there are more guests than menu items, have some bring wine, cocktail makings, or flowers for the table.

If you want to stage the entire event yourself, making everything from scratch, your menu choices are as wide as the sky. No law says you have to stick to traditional menus. Serve lasagne at Christmas if you want to, or stir-fried cashew chicken at Thanksgiving. On the other hand, if you love the culinary traditions of the holidays, rest assured that a traditional dinner can be one of the simplest meals to make. At Thanksgiving, for example, the classic elements, from roast turkey to pumpkin pie, are as easy as—well—pie, if you just stick to the basics. Remember, too, that when you embark on a cooking project such as Thanksgiving dinner, you always have help close at hand, ranging from relatives

Don't overwhelm guests with a bird that's too large for the group that has gathered.

to newspaper and magazine articles, classic cookbooks, and cooking sites on the World Wide Web (see page 143).

There's also room for variations on the theme. For instance, consider cooking an unstuffed turkey in a covered grill. The weather needn't be balmy enough for a picnic—just warm enough for you to set up the grill in a sheltered spot and check the bird's progress now and then. Put a pan in the bottom of the grill, with hot coals banked at either end so the bird cooks by indirect heat. Set the turkey on a rack, 4 to 6 inches (10–15cm) above the pan, and baste it with the drippings about every half hour. If it's looking too brown before it's done, cover it with aluminum foil. Besides producing a moist, smoke-flavored turkey, cooking on a grill frees up the oven for side dishes and desserts.

TIMING

For first-time turkey chefs, the most frequent mistake is allowing too little time. A frozen turkey needs at least two days to thaw in the refrigerator (never thaw it on the kitchen counter; it's like throwing an open house for bacteria). Place the turkey in a plastic bag or on a large plate in the fridge so the juices won't come into contact with other food. Before cooking, rinse the turkey—inside and out—under cold running water and pat dry. Always wash your hands with soap and water for 20 seconds before and after handling raw poultry; any utensils and cutting boards that were used in preparing the raw turkey should also be washed with soap and water immediately.

A 13- to 15-pound (5.8–6.8kg) turkey will serve six to eight healthy eaters, with enough for leftovers. Roasting takes anywhere from three hours for a 10-pounder (4.5kg) without stuffing to five and a half hours for a stuffed 24-pound (10.8kg) monster. For more-specific times, check any comprehensive cookbook or call the U.S. Department of Agriculture's meat and poultry hotline (page 143). Cooking the stuffing outside the bird will allow a shorter roasting time and ensure that both

A Holiday Dinner

---※---

ORCHESTRATING A HOLIDAY FEAST is easier than you think. The key is organization and scheduling. Below is a countdown to a dinner of roast turkey, stuffing, gravy, mashed potatoes, a vegetable casserole, a salad, and dinner rolls, followed by pie with whipped cream. The stuffing is cooked outside the bird, to give you a shorter roasting time and ensure that both are thoroughly done when you serve.

...one month out. Plan your menu; make your shopping list; take an inventory of china, silver, glassware, and serving pieces.

...two weeks prior. Buy nonperishable food: flour, spices, canned pumpkin, and frozen turkey and vegetables. Buy nonperishable beverages such as wine, liquor, and mixers.

...one week prior. Wash any serving pieces, glassware, silverware, carving knives, pitchers, or plates that you haven't used lately.

...three days prior. Buy perishable foods such as potatoes, vegetables for the casserole and salad, and any staples such as eggs or milk. Begin thawing frozen turkey in refrigerator.

...two days prior. Buy fresh turkey (if not using frozen) and refrigerate; shop for supplies such as ice, rolls, and fresh herbs.

...one day prior. Make pies; clean house.

...six to eight hours before serving. Set table. Make hors d'oeuvres and refrigerate.

...three to five hours before serving. Make vegetable casserole and salad and refrigerate. Prepare turkey and put it into the oven to roast, basting it periodically. (See note.)

...one and a half hours before. Make broth with giblets; prepare stuffing and put it in the oven; peel and chop potatoes and put them on the stove to steam.

...one hour before. Prepare salad dressing; arrange premade hors d'oeuvres on platters and set them out for guests. Remove premade vegetable casserole from the refrigerator.

...30 minutes before. Check thermometer to see how quickly turkey is cooking; transfer stuffing to serving dish and keep warm; mash potatoes, cover, and keep warm.

...20 minutes before. Remove turkey from oven and let stand; baste turkey with pan juices; leave oven on to warm rolls and heat vegetable casserole. Put away appetizers.

...10 minutes before. Remove rolls from oven; cover and keep warm; uncork red wine if you're serving it; fill water glasses; set out butter; toss salad with dressing. Make gravy.

...immediately before serving. Transfer turkey to serving platter; transfer gravy to a gravy bowl; reheat stuffing, if necessary; transfer potatoes to serving dish; set out vegetable casserole, salad, rolls, and relish.

...after main course. Clear away plates and serving dishes and set out dessert plates; make coffee and tea; whip cream; offer dessert.

Note: Adjust the cooking times according to individual recipes and the size of your turkey. Depending on your oven temperature, the turkey may take slightly more or less time to cook; start checking it at least a half hour before you expect it to be done.

bird and stuffing are done when you eat them. If you're feeding a big crowd, roasting two small turkeys instead of one big one will also speed up the roasting process.

Oven and barbecue temperatures vary, so begin checking your turkey using an instant-read thermometer a half hour before estimated finishing time. It's done if the thermometer reads at least 180°F (82°C) when inserted in the thickest part of the thigh—without touching the bone. Meat that is a bit pink is fine if the bird has reached this temperature, but juices should run clear, not pink. The center of any stuffing inside the turkey should reach a temperature of 165°F (74°C); when both turkey and stuffing are done, remove the stuffing from the bird immediately.

Encourage relatives *to bring their specialties to your holiday dinner. Grandma would be proud to prepare a favorite family recipe.*

THE GAME PLAN

Once the turkey is in the oven or on the grill, the rest will fall into place easily. If you've prepared side dishes ahead of time so you don't have to stay in the kitchen, take everyone out to play for an hour or two—longer if you're cooking a big bird, but make sure someone looks in on it every half hour or so. Whether you have a rousing game of touch football or simply go for a long walk, you'll cut down on predinner snacking and drinking, thus leaving appetites sufficiently whetted to appreciate your handiwork to the fullest.

How much of the predinner preparation you hand off to others only you can decide. In some families, it makes sense to delegate large parts of this. In others, it causes more stress than it's worth. If you're a gregarious cook with a big kitchen and a crowd of eager and capable helpers, have everyone pitch in. Or start a tradition that whoever cooks doesn't clean up. Maybe the women in the family can cook one year, the men the next. Give the kids whatever chores you feel they're up to. Folding napkins is always safe, and if your children are small, have grown-ups handle any breakables. Toward cocktail hour, set up a bar in the living room, with baskets of munchies, and assign someone to keep it stocked. This will ease traffic in the kitchen as you deal with last-minute details.

While you wait for the bird to cook, have a rousing game of touch football or take a long walk. You'll cut down on predinner snacking.

ON THE LIGHTER SIDE

---✳---

THOUGH THE BIG FAMILY DINNER GETS MOST OF THE ATTENTION AT HOLIDAY TIME, IT'S FAR FROM THE ONLY CULINARY GAME IN TOWN. YOU MAY BE LOOKING FOR ALTERNATIVES TO THE TRADITIONAL HOST-DOES-IT-ALL FEAST.

Or you may be seeking creative ways to use the leftovers that it generates. Stay-over guests will also need to be fed before and after the holiday. Here are some ideas that will provide maximum fun with minimum fuss, whether it's having a potluck or tossing together a quick meal.

THE HOLIDAY POTLUCK

It was good enough for the pilgrims that first Thanksgiving in Massachusetts, and it'll work just as well for you on Christmas, New Year's Day, Passover, or Easter. If you want to entertain on a big scale without doing all the cooking, invite the gang for potluck. When estimating quantities, the rules of thumb are the same as they are for a sit-down dinner (see page 91).

But don't get carried away with making sure everything comes out even—nobody ever lapsed into malnutrition from one unbalanced meal. Just give your guests some general guidelines (entrée, salad, or dessert) and, within those parameters, have them bring whatever they consider the star of their culinary repertoire.

The concept works especially well with a ceremonial meal like a Passover seder. For example, if your mother has an heirloom recipe for light-as-air matzo balls, have her bring the makings for matzo ball soup. Ask your uncle to make his famous knishes, and assign to your sister the job of creating an updated version of the whipped sweet potatoes with pineapple and marshmallows that you used to adore as children. Your

Most guests will be happy to contribute
to your holiday dinner.

aunt can bring some Passover wine; your father, the family prayer books, or Haggadoth. Even the busiest guest on your list can take on the task of making the *haroseth*, symbolizing the mortar for the bricks the slaves made in Egypt: The usual ingredients are chopped apples and walnuts mixed together with sweet red Passover wine. Children can help you prepare the other symbolic foods and set them out on the ceremonial plate. All that's left for you to do is to prepare the main course, traditionally chicken or brisket.

A NOSHING CHRISTMAS

Whether you cook it all yourself or you have a lot of help, pulling off a large-scale dinner is one thing on Thanksgiving, when almost everyone's attention is focused on food and the blessings of the year just past. It's a whole different story at Christmas,

Best Behavior

To head off disagreements at the family holiday dinner—and to help your children develop good table manners more quickly—invite a nonrelative to join you: a college student who's far from home, a single friend without family, or a business associate. You'll find that family behavior can improve magically in the presence of an outsider.

and the holiday setting. Set out the food and keep a pot of mulled wine simmering on the stove. Then everyone can sip and munch when the mood strikes. If it has snowed recently, go outside for a romp,

Instead of planning a meal, invite everyone in the family to come bearing a few hors d'oeuvres. You provide the drinks and the setting.

when you are surrounded by grown-ups who are starting to feel the extra pounds left by a month of holiday parties, and by kids so excited with their just-opened presents that they can scarcely sit still long enough to eat a bowl of cereal, much less mind their manners at the dinner table for what feels to them like eternity. If you're beginning to wonder why you even bother to cook dinner on Christmas, maybe this is the year to try something different.

Instead of planning a big meal, invite everyone in the family to come bearing a few hors d'oeuvres. You provide the drinks

complete with a snow sculpture contest with prizes for the best snow dogs or snow bunnies. The kids will get to burn some energy, free from the worry of having to behave themselves at the table (they can practice their etiquette at Thanksgiving), and the grown-ups will get to recapture the feeling of childhood Christmases, when there was a lot of playing to be done and almost no work. Perhaps more important to some of the adults, they'll be freer to resist the temptations of one more holiday table laden with food crying, "Eat me now. Worry about your waistline tomorrow."

To allow everybody the greatest freedom of movement—and control over their calorie intake—limit the fare to finger food. Simple treats such as fruit wedges skewered on toothpicks, shrimp wrapped in fresh basil leaves (available year-round at supermarkets), tiny pâté sandwiches on cocktail-size rye bread, and minimuffins—sweet and savory—are easy to eat on the move.

Yet another advantage to a noshing Christmas—or its close cousin, the buffet—is that if you plan it far enough in advance, it provides a great opportunity to use up Thanksgiving leftovers. Instead of joining the shopping crowds on the first official day of the holiday season, stay home and recycle your turkey into cocktail-size burritos, turnovers, or tiny shepherd's pies. Then tuck them into the freezer so they'll be on hand for Christmas Day or anytime unexpected guests drop by and you want fast but substantial cocktail fare. If you lack the time or the patience for cooking so soon after the big feast, simply remove the turkey meat from the bone and freeze it in small portions that you can pull out as needed for sandwiches, salads, pots of chili, or any recipes that call for turkey or chicken. Don't overlook other Thanksgiving leftovers. Cranberries that you didn't use in recipes the day before can go into muffins, tarts, or cookies—or get whirled into a

If you love *Chinese food, try serving it straight from the boxes for easy cleanup at a New Year party.*

fruit smoothie. You can also use eggnog in baking: Substitute it for milk in any cake, quick bread, or cookie recipe.

THE HOLIDAY BRUNCH

Another easy, cost-effective get-together is the holiday brunch. Like the noshing Christmas, it also provides more potential for activity than the average sit-down dinner. For one thing, it's early enough in the day that you'll have time and energy left over to play afterward. Have a New Year's Day brunch for the family, then go for an afternoon of cross-country skiing. Make Easter brunch the kickoff for the big egg hunt. Most brunch fare, such as thick French toast or fruit-filled pancakes topped with fresh Vermont maple syrup, is quick and easy to make. You can make the dishes weeks in advance, freeze them, and simply warm them up when the time comes. Quiches also freeze well, and you can fill them with virtually anything edible. The base is the same for any quiche (eggs, light cream or half-and-half, salt, pepper, and nutmeg to taste). Follow the proportions in any comprehensive cookbook, then add any meats, cheese, fish, or vegetables you find appealing, and pour the mixture into a pie shell (homemade or store-bought and frozen) that's been baked for about 15 minutes. It's a great way to use all those

EASY BUFFET MEALS

✳

THE HOLIDAY FEAST NEEDN'T BE a sit-down ordeal of fidgety youngsters and bumping elbows. Serve it buffet-style and let your guests sit wherever they like. A buffet is also ideal for feeding a crowd of houseguests before and after the holiday.

▲ **Fresh fruit** *completes an Easter brunch. Serve it with miniature pastries.*

◀ **Leftover turkey** *and stuffing make an instant day-after-Thanksgiving lunch.*

▲ **A salad** *of precut lettuce, fruit, and pecans is impressive but easy to include in a buffet.*

▲ **Rather than cook** *eggs to order for a holiday brunch, make a giant frittata using leftover vegetables or meats.*

You'll have more time *to enjoy the company of your guests if you rely on premade foods. Prepare these yourself ahead of time or pick them up at a deli or gourmet market.*

odd bits of leftovers that are too small for any other use, and any combination you like will work just fine. Try leftover hamburger with cheddar cheese and scallions; salmon with peas; or Swiss cheese with leftover salad. (Day-old salad, wilted with dressing and baked into a quiche, rolled

the fruit salad in a bowl, mix a pitcher of mimosas (use one part orange juice to one part champagne), pull a quiche from the freezer and pop it into the oven, and put the French bread in to warm it up. Brew a pot of coffee, and you're ready for your first gathering of the new year.

INSTANT REPASTS

Even without a freezer full of leftovers, it's easy to turn out last-minute meals when unexpected guests stay for dinner or when

One of your most trustworthy tools is the bagged salad mixture. Along with crusty bread and fine wine, it can transform the humblest entrée.

into an omelet, or broiled inside a chicken-and-melted-cheese sandwich, is one of the world's most underrated pleasures.)

For an almost instant New Year's Day brunch, stop at the market on your way home from work on New Year's Eve and pick up a premade fruit salad, French bread, fresh-squeezed orange juice, and some champagne. The next morning, put

you have to feed the family in a hurry before the Christmas play rehearsal. One of your most trustworthy tools—and one of the most useful items supermarkets have added to their repertoire in the last few years—is the bagged salad mixture. All you have to do is add your favorite bottled dressing. (These, too, get better all the time.) Not only will a fancy salad mix save you time when you need it most, but along with store-bought crusty bread warmed in the oven, a bottle of fine wine, and fresh fruit for dessert, it can also turn the humblest entrée into a dinner fit for your boss, your new neighbors, or your houseguests from out of town.

EASY ENTRÉES

Any time you want an entrée that looks as good as anything you could spend hours preparing, boil a pot of linguine and toss it with premade pesto and halved cherry tomatoes. Put a chunk of Parmesan cheese on a plate with a small grater and let your guests grate their own. It tastes better, and the leftover cheese will stay fresh longer than if you grate it all at once. (For greatest longevity, store it wrapped in plastic.)

Or try this more casual idea: Fill a colorful assortment of red, yellow, orange, and green peppers with canned chili, shred some cheddar on top, and arrange them in a baking dish. If you're in a hurry to eat, put them in the microwave for the recommended length of time, but for better flavor, set them in your oven to bake for 45 minutes while you turn your attention to other matters—such as viewing that holiday TV special with your family.

One of the greatest labor-saving foods of all—and one that's sure to please even the pickiest child or most allergy-prone adult—is the common baked potato. The purists among us shun the microwave, preferring to bake spuds in the oven, without foil, so the skin stays crispy, but it's your call. Whichever method you choose, split them open when they're done and serve them on a platter surrounded by bowls of easy toppings: chopped onions and green peppers, salsa from a jar, shredded cheddar cheese, and store-bought tuna salad. For a more impressive presentation with only a little more effort, slice off the top of each baked potato; then scoop out the insides. Combine them in a bowl with premade pesto, minced garlic, ground black pepper, a splash of milk, and some freshly grated Parmesan, and stuff the mixture back inside the potato shells. Sprinkle Parmesan over the tops and put them in the microwave for a few minutes to warm the stuffing. As an alternative, bake the potatoes in the oven for another half hour—the flavors will blend better that way and the cheese on top will brown nicely.

A note of caution before you set about stocking your pantry and collecting cook-ahead recipes: Producing meals with more flair than fuss can be habit forming.

Breakfast for Dinner

When the combination of work, seasonal chores, and holiday fun leaves you little time for cooking, serve the family breakfast for dinner. Homemade waffles are just as delicious and fast to make in the evening as they are in the morning. Serve them with real maple syrup, orange juice, and slices of melon. You'll like the ease and the speed; the kids will love the novelty.

HOSTING a holiday
Gathering

—✳—

1 Entertain only when you want to; If you need to throw a party because of business obligations, turn the chores over to an **event planner.** **2** Give guests at least a month's notice, if only in the form of save-the-date **announcements.** **3** Reserve rental equipment and book professionals such as caterers and musicians as far in **advance** as you can. **4** If you're staging the party yourself, call on **friends** and family to help with the event. **5** Stockpile frozen casseroles and **quick-fix** ingredients so you can feed extra guests in a pinch. **6** Assume that people will eat and drink **more** than you expect, and buy more of everything than you think you'll need. **7** Entertain at nonpeak times, such as at **brunch** or after dinner, when people have more free time. **8** Plan gatherings around holiday **events** such as pageants and concerts, or activities such as tree trimming. **9** If you're planning a year-end **office party,** ask the staff how they'd like to celebrate. ●

Easy Entertaining

SIMPLE WAYS TO MAKE
YOUR PARTIES SPARKLE

* —— * —— *

Whether they're business soirees or casual gatherings with old friends, parties are a big part of everyone's life between Thanksgiving and New Year's Eve. The glamorous galas, the joyous family get-togethers—these are the stuff of which wonderful memories are made. For many people, they are also the stuff of which tension headaches are made.

Even if you're a dedicated party animal, entertaining at holiday time can be stressful. Especially during this season, people have great expectations of sumptuous food, sparkling music, and lavish decor. With all the other demands at this time of year, you may not feel up to the challenge.

But if you relax, leave perfection to Hollywood set designers, and follow a few simple guidelines, you can enjoy every party you give for exactly what it is—a chance for you and your guests to have fun and to bask in congenial company.

PLANNING THE PARTY

———— ✳ ————

THE FIRST RULE OF ENTERTAINING—AT ANY TIME OF YEAR—IS DON'T DO IT UNLESS YOU WANT TO. IF BUSINESS OBLIGATIONS FORCE YOU TO HOST A GATHERING YOU DON'T HAVE TIME FOR, FARM OUT THE WORK TO SOMEONE ELSE.

Hold your event at a restaurant or hotel where you can communicate your budget and other details to a professional planner, and let that person take it from there.

But if you've decided to do it by yourself, throwing a holiday party needn't be a major trauma. Here are some guidelines that will make life easier when you're staging the event on your own:

Plan ahead. For the best turnout at year-end holiday time or during the busy summer months, try to give your guests at least a month's notice. You don't have to send formal announcements—phone calls, postcards, or e-mail asking people to save the date will do fine. Later you can follow up with invitations noting specifics such as time, location, and what the main activity will be—whether it's trimming your Christmas tree or splashing in your pool on the Fourth of July.

If you'll be renting a party site or hiring musicians, book as far in advance as you can. Both are in the greatest demand between Thanksgiving and New Year's Eve and during the summer wedding season. So if you want a room at the country club for your Christmas party, a big rented tent

Plan your party to allow plenty of food and drink
and enough room for guests to sit.

for a Father's Day fete in June, or a square-dance band for your Fourth of July barbecue, get your order in early. (See page 140 for a planning checklist.)

Get help. Even if you've resolved to do it yourself, don't go it alone. The more aid you rally to your side, the more smoothly the process will go—and the more fun it will be. At a large gathering, having a teenager to help out with the kitchen chores can make a big difference in your morale. Hire your neighbors' son or your teenage niece to help clean glassware or serve appetizers. Or do a little holiday bartering. Call your friend who makes fabulous hors d'oeuvres and tell her that if she whips up a trayful for your tree-trimming party, you'll make your famous amaretto cheesecake bars for her New Year's Eve soiree. Ask your neighbor the tenor to sing sentimental Irish songs at your Saint Patrick's Day gathering, and lend him your recordings of John Philip Sousa marches for his Fourth of July barbecue.

Expect the unexpected. Every experienced host knows that throwing a party means strolling into the great unknown. The possibilities for mishap are endless. A windstorm could douse the power in the middle of your Christmas videothon, leaving your guests staring at a darkened screen and your soufflé falling flat in the oven. Your energetic dog could skid into the barbecue during your Fourth of July cookout, sending your T-bone steaks flying into the petunia bed.

At times like these it pays to have two weapons at your disposal: a sense of humor and backup resources. If you've laid

Stocking the Bar

Even if you know your guests aren't big drinkers, it pays not to get caught short. A rule of thumb is to expect that each guest will consume two glasses of wine, two bottles of beer, or two mixed drinks per hour. Also allow between a quarter and a half pound (125–250g) of ice cubes and two or three beverage glasses per guest.

in a stash of candles and stocked your kitchen with quick-fix ingredients such as salad makings, crackers, cheeses, and pâté, you'll be ready for any emergency.

SIZING UP THE PARTY

Even barring disasters, you'll find that your party will flow much more smoothly if you assume that it won't go exactly as planned. Anticipate that people will eat and drink more than you expect, and shop accordingly—buy more of everything than you think you'll need. It's far more pleasant to have to put away leftovers than to let your guests go hungry—or to have to call out for an emergency pizza.

If you feel a distinct twinge in your wallet when you realize how much all the food and drink will cost (both will always cost more than you think), you might want to lower your sights. Instead of having 50 people for your New Year's Eve party, invite 25. You'll be able to relax and enjoy

HOLIDAY PARTY TIMETABLE

--- ✳ ---

L IFE CAN GET HECTIC during the year-end holiday season, so when you're planning a party it pays to have guidelines for scheduling. Here's a task-by-task guide to organizing your event, whether it's a Christmas or Hanukkah open house or a New Year's Eve party.

	2–6 weeks before	3–7 days before	24 hours before	Few hours before
PLANNING				
Choose the site, date, and party activity (if any)	●			
Send invitations	●			
Hire professional helpers or recruit volunteers; assign tasks	●			
Plan food and bar menus	●			
SHOPPING				
Check inventory of party equipment and supplies	●			
Buy equipment, supplies, and nonperishable food and drink	●			
Shop for perishable groceries			●	
Pick up flowers, purchase premade foods			●	
Buy last-minute supplies such as ice				●
COOKING				
Finalize the menu	●			
Assign potluck dishes (if any)	●			
Prepare make-ahead foods for freezing	●			
Prepare make-ahead foods to refrigerate			●	
Cut up ingredients for salads			●	
Thaw premade frozen dishes in the refrigerator			●	
Prepare last-minute dishes				●
SETUP				
Wash china and glassware		●		
Assemble music tapes or CDs		●		
Clean bathrooms and kitchen			●	
Pick up or receive rented equipment			●	
Arrange flowers and decorations			●	
Set up the bar			●	
Set up buffet tables			●	
Fill serving dishes with nonperishable foods and set out				●
Chill white wine, champagne, beer, and soft drinks on ice				●

your party a lot more if you're not fretting about how you're going to stretch the budget to pay for everything.

SCHEDULING

When you're planning parties between Thanksgiving and New Year's, which for most people is the busiest part of the year, think beyond the obvious times. Instead of trying to corral a full evening on guests' already dense calendars—and preparing a full evening's worth of food, drink, and activities—why not get people together on a weekend morning or afternoon, or perhaps some evening after dinner?

Invite friends in for breakfast on Saturday before you head out on your shopping quests. Serve something easy like a Swiss-style continental breakfast of crusty hard rolls bought at the bakery; pots of jam and preserves; a platter of fresh fruit; a pot of coffee, tea, or hot chocolate; and a plate of good cheese. (Any kind will do, but if you want real Swiss varieties, look in a supermarket or cheese shop for Appenzeller, Emmentaler, Gruyère, Royalp, or raclette.) The bread and cheese will give people stamina for the day's rounds, rather than the immediate but short-lived kick they'd get from sweet pastries. While you nibble, compare time-saving strategies and simple gift ideas—you might all find yourselves inspired as well as energized.

Or try an end-of-the-shopping-day get-together. Compare notes about your finds over well-earned cocktails and frozen miniature egg rolls you can warm up in minutes in the oven or the microwave. If the group seems out of sorts after battling

Your guests will be *more relaxed and convivial if you schedule your party for an off-peak time, such as after dinner.*

the crowds, watching a favorite Christmas movie (see the list on page 134) may help take everyone's mind off holiday pressures.

Instead of inviting people to a dinner party during the year-end holiday period, invite them for dessert, coffee, and after-dinner port. You'll find people are more likely to accept when they don't have to commit to a whole evening in the midst of the holiday rush. This is also easier on your budget than serving a full meal, and unless you want to make dessert for the occasion rather than buying it or taking it from your freezer, the only last-minute work involved is making the coffee. The after-dinner hour is also an ideal time for spontaneous entertaining. Call neighbors in the afternoon and ask them to drop by. Watch a holiday video, play a game, or just enjoy a leisurely chat.

HOLIDAY PARTY THEMES

───── ✳ ─────

YOU NEVER NEED AN EXCUSE TO GIVE A PARTY. BUT DURING THE HOLIDAYS, WHEN ALMOST EVERY TOWN COMES ALIVE WITH PARADES, PAGEANTS, OR FIREWORKS DISPLAYS, IT'S EASY TO BUILD PARTIES AROUND THESE EVENTS.

Even holiday chores such as pumpkin carving or tree trimming can be springboards to festivity. Focusing your gathering on an activity can also help simplify your role as host: With your guests' attention directed toward the action, you don't have to work as hard to entertain them.

FALL AND WINTER

When the weather turns cool, the social whirl picks up for just about everyone. Through the fall and into the winter, it sometimes seems that party invitations

Kwanzaa is a time *for families to celebrate their African heritage. On the last night of the holiday, gather for a potluck featuring favorite Kwanzaa dishes.*

drift through the mail slot like leaves floating from the trees. If you feel that yet another party where everyone stands around drinking would prove boring for your guests, try one of these variations:

Tree-trimming party. This is especially fun if you're a true ornament connoisseur with a collection that never fails to draw oohs and aahs when people gather around your tree. A party centered around adorning the tree gives everyone a chance to admire your mini-artworks up close. It's also a great way to entertain friends who love Christmas decorating but lack the space or the inclination to have their own trees. Devotees of festive tree trimmings like to hold them on the night of the midwinter solstice, which falls on either December 21

or 22, depending on the year. In the original western European solstice celebrations, people brought evergreen trees into their houses, decking them with sweets to ensure good things in the year to come and with candles and disc-shaped ornaments to represent the sun's return to the winter sky.

ENJOYING THE PARTY

When guests arrive, have your tree in its stand and the lights in place so guests can devote their time to the more enjoyable task of decking the tree with ornaments. Unpack the ones you want to use and set them in baskets or trays lined with colorful cloth or tissue paper. You'll save your guests the bother of rooting through the ornament boxes, and you won't have to be concerned about any breakage that might result. If your collection includes treasured heirlooms whose demise would ruin your evening, put them in a separate place and hang them yourself later.

Serve mulled wine and assorted finger foods, either purchased or pulled out of your freezer and heated, so your guests can drink and nibble as they decorate.

Hold That Candle

When preparing for your candle-lit caroling party, be sure to buy dripless candles to prevent hot wax from burning hands. For added protection, any time you'll be holding a candle in your hand, slip a bobeche onto it, just above hand height. These circular paper or metal collars are available at craft shops or at many houseware and hardware stores.

dishes for your guests to bring, such as hoppin' John (black-eyed peas with rice) or a sweet-potato casserole. You'll find recipes in the many Kwanzaa cookbooks available at bookstores, and on World Wide Web sites (see page 143).

Christmas caroling. There are few better ways to meet new neighbors and reconnect with others you haven't seen in a while. Rally a congenial group and wander from door to door, candles in hand.

Building your gathering around an activity focuses your guests' attention so you don't have to work as hard to entertain them.

Kwanzaa party. African Americans have joined in this December observance since its inception in 1966, and its popularity has soared in recent years. Share its meaning and symbolism with a few good friends by inviting them to celebrate with your family on the last night of Kwanzaa. Make it a modified potluck and suggest specific

You don't have to sound like Bing Crosby; you just have to enjoy lifting your voices in song and bringing good cheer to others. Make copies of the song lyrics for everyone so no one's left humming through any of the verses. And if someone you know is an accomplished musician, appoint him or her conductor. As you depart from each house, invite its residents to join you, and end the parade at your place, where you have a big pot of soup or stew warming on the stove; baskets of bread, cheese, and apples for munching; and some hearty red wine for toasting good fellowship.

HOLIDAY FUN

Latke tasting. If you stick to the basics, Hanukkah is about as simple as holidays get. But there are easy ways to make it more fun. One is a latke (potato pancake) tasting. Invite each of your guests to bring the makings for a new twist on this traditional Hanukkah fare: sweet potato latkes, 'Yukon Gold' latkes served with pear sauce on the side instead of the usual applesauce, latkes with shredded beets and onions, latkes made from blue potatoes and shredded

Lighting the menorah *on the last night of Hanukkah can be the prelude to a party featuring dreidel games and homemade latkes.*

red and yellow peppers. Everyone can take turns at the food processor and the griddle. Your friends will get to show off their creative culinary skills, and you'll be able to spend more time chatting with your guests instead of tending the stove.

Fun-in-the-snow party. Invite friends out for an afternoon of skating, sledding, or cross-country skiing in a nearby park. Then return to your house for dinner. Have some hot cider or hot buttered rum to sip, and cheese and crackers to munch on while a premade casserole warms in the oven and a salad awaits tossing.

Pre-event party. Before heading off to your town's tree-lighting ceremony or the Christmas pageant or carol service at church, have everyone over for a simple dinner—perhaps a no-fuss Mexican meal of enchilada casserole, warm store-bought tortillas, chips with jars of salsa and guacamole. Come back afterward for coffee or hot chocolate and a simple dessert.

Cookie decorating party. This is a fun theme for guests old and young. The day before, bake a few large batches of gingerbread or sugar cookies cut into holiday shapes. Remember to poke a hole in the top of each cookie before baking—this will let your guests hang the cookies from their trees at home. Have white and colored icing on hand, along with chocolate chips, raisins, and red and green sprinkles. You can make pastry bags in a pinch by cutting a small hole in one corner of plastic sandwich bags—squeeze the icing out through the hole. Serve nutritious snacks such as cheese, crackers, and raw vegetables so your guests don't fill up on cookies.

HOLIDAY CENTERPIECES

✳

S IMPLE YET DRAMATIC FOCAL POINTS such as these can bring holiday magic to your dinner table or buffet. Start with a serving bowl or large platter, then add props—candy, flowers, fruit, or other objects—that invoke the spirit of the season.

▲ **Party favors** *become the centerpiece for a pre-Christmas dinner party. Or simply wrap empty boxes for a festive look.*

▼ **On New Year's Day,** *adorn your table with pineapples, symbols of hospitality.*

▲ **Fill a bowl** *with gold Christmas orna-ments (or artificial fruit sprayed with gold paint), then tuck in pink pepper berries to cascade over the sides. The berries are avail-able from florists year-round.*

▼ **At a Hanukkah party,** *place a big bowl of dreidels and chocolate coins where guests can pick up the dreidels and start playing.*

A costume party is easy on the host:
The guests provide the entertainment.

New Year's Eve mystery party. Instead of the usual stand-around-and-drink party, invite a group of mystery fans to help you enact a murder investigation based on a kit you buy in a game store. Don't get the wrong idea—these are not macabre horror stories; nor are they action-packed, shoot-'em-up thrillers. Rather, they're decidedly nongory, intellectually challenging whodunits in the Agatha Christie vein. The kits include invitations that give complete profiles of all the characters involved—the victim, the murderer, the detectives, and the witnesses—as well as relevant information such as who knows what about whom. You assign each guest a role, which you describe in your invitation. He or she comes dressed as the assigned character and prepared to act the part, which could be that of a foreign correspondent in World War II Paris, a poet in 13th-century China, or a grieving widow in 1930's England. As the plot unfolds, the characters try to preserve their supposedly pristine reputations while letting everyone else know the secrets they've found out about all of the others. Telling outright untruths is not allowed, but creative evasion is strongly encouraged. Let the characters get acquainted over cocktails. Then, after the collected assembly has fingered the culprit, pop the champagne corks to celebrate the triumph of justice and the start of a brand-new year.

SPRING AND SUMMER

Planning your gathering around a holiday event works just as well in spring and summer as it does in autumn and winter. Invite guests to join you for your town's Easter parade, then head to your place for a quick brunch of quiche and muffins, juice, and coffee. Or invite the neighbors over for grilled hamburgers before you head off to view Fourth of July fireworks.

On Saint Patrick's Day, rally the gang for some Irish pub grub—Irish soda bread, smoked salmon, cheddar or blarney cheese, and pickled onions—washed down with pints of Guinness stout or shots of Irish whiskey. Then hop in a cab and head for an Irish folk concert. Finish off the evening with a round of Irish coffee.

The long-weekend holidays of late spring and summer—Memorial Day, Independence Day, and Labor Day—seem made for laid-back outdoor get-togethers. Why not cultivate that relaxed, even lazy, mood with an outdoor open house? Fire up the charcoal grill, get out the ice-cream maker (or rent one), set up the badminton net and the croquet wickets, spread out the pool gear, and invite your friends and neighbors to come and go at their leisure.

PARTIES FOR KIDS

Few sights could be more heartwarming than a party of gleeful toddlers dressed in their holiday best, entranced by the decorations, delighted by the yummy food, and giggling at the grown-ups who are clowning for their amusement.

And few parties could be more draining than one spent running after toddlers who've decided that the Christmas tree is meant for climbing, cleaning up spilled apple juice, patting the backs of those who gulp their cookies a little too fast, or comforting those who burst into tears at the sight of Halloween ghosts and goblins or that scary, bearded man with the bright red suit and the loud laugh.

If for no reason other than keeping your serenity and good humor intact, it's usually best to confine your kids' parties to ages four and above. But once they hit

NO HOLIDAY PARTY WOULD BE COMPLETE WITHOUT FESTIVE BEVERAGES. THESE ARE EASY TO SERVE AND SURE TO PLEASE.

Punches

Spiked or unspiked, holiday punches are endless in their variety—and since guests help themselves, you're freed from bartending duty. Borrow or rent a punch bowl and glasses, and look in on the punch now and then to replenish ice and fruit garnishes.

Hot drinks

After an evening of ice-skating or caroling, hot beverages warm guests' hands while reviving flagging energy. Eggnog, hot chocolate, hot apple cider (served with a stick of cinnamon), mulled wine, and wassail are traditional favorites that are hard to beat.

Wines, spirits, and liqueurs

Even if you don't drink much during the rest of the year, Christmas Eve is the time to open cherished bottles of brandy, sherry, or homemade wine or liqueur to sip while you gaze at the burning Yule log.

Sparkling beverages

Celebrate the close of another year by breaking out the champagne—or sparkling cider for kids, nondrinkers, and designated drivers. Or mix fruit juice with sparkling mineral water and optional alcohol, and decorate with citrus slices or strips.

grade-school age, most children are intrepid party animals, and they're great fun to be around at holiday time.

For just about anybody between 5 and 12, Halloween ranks high on the holiday calendar. If your kids are like most, they'd probably love a classic costume party, complete with bobbing for apples and a jack-o'-lantern contest (draw faces with paints, as knives in young hands can be a serious

cookies) or gray gelatin molded in the shape of a brain. For truly ghoulish children, hand out lollipops with real, edible insects inside. Brain molds and bug candy are available at novelty stores or by mail; see the list on page 142 for a source.

Once the teen years arrive, acceptance of much detailed party planning by adults goes out the window; but teenagers almost universally love activity-based parties, and

Entertaining kids for an afternoon makes a great gift for other parents, who can use the time to prepare for their own holiday revelries.

hazard). Give prizes for the best costumes—most original, prettiest, ugliest, most realistic—and serve appropriately disgusting food like candy gummy worms in a big jar of "dirt" (made of crumbled-up chocolate

Entertain young goblins *and wizards with a Halloween party featuring "ghastly" foods. Award prizes for the costumes deemed scariest, most original, and most beautiful.*

they'll gladly accept help (and financial backing) to throw them. Chances are you'll win a parent-of-the-year contest if you rent a skating rink (ice or roller) for a Halloween party. Make sure you specify the activity on the invitations so guests can choose costumes that allow freedom of movement. When they've all skated to their hearts' content, take the whole gang to your place for pizzas and soft drinks.

At Christmastime, when the child in all of us rises to the surface, it's especially fun to be around kids. Entertaining them for an afternoon makes a great gift for other parents, who can use time alone to prepare for or recover from their own holiday revelries. Once you know their tastes, kids are easy to feed (ask their parents for suggestions if you need to), and they appreciate small details like fancy cookies from the bakery. Try these ideas:

A party for the birds. Make a Christmas tree for your feathered neighbors. The tree can be one growing in your yard or the one in your living room to which the time has come to bid adieu. (Simply remove all the trimmings and anchor it against an outdoor tree by tying cord around both trunks.) Assemble the makings of gourmet bird cuisine—pinecones and peanut butter to stuff inside them, sunflower seeds to stick into clumps of suet, and cranberries and popcorn to string into garlands. Then have fun making avian snacks and bedecking the tree.

Kids' New Year's Eve. If you can't find a babysitter on the biggest party night of the year, invite your kids' friends over and throw a party for them yourself. Their parents will appreciate the favor and perhaps do the same for you next year. You can take them to some afternoon and early evening events if your town has a First Night celebration, as upward of 200 towns do across the United States and Canada. All First Night schedules include performances and activities aimed at youngsters, ranging from puppet shows, parades, and face painting to theater productions. At

Channeling Youthful Energy

Kids need a balance between free play and structured activities. When you're entertaining a group of children, plan just a few activities and make sure there are times during the party when they can do what they like. Have some alternative activities in case someone doesn't want to participate in the main event.

home, before small heads start to droop too much, throw confetti, blow whistles, and toast the New Year with sparkling cider. (It might be only 9 P.M. at your place, but it's midnight somewhere, even if it's just a ship at sea.)

Easter at the zoo. Take a group of kids to the local zoo. These days zoos are active breeding grounds for endangered species of every kind, and in the spring you are apt to find infants and still-babyish yearlings that will delight children of all ages. Chances are you'll also find a hands-on area where everyone can pet sheep, goats, baby pigs, and best of all, lots of bunnies. Rather than lug a lunch, treat everyone to hot dogs, ice cream, and soft drinks from the refreshment stands.

THE OFFICE PARTY

In large companies, the annual holiday party tends to be a lavish affair, where professionals handle everything from decorating the site to writing the boss's final heartfelt toast. All the employees need to do is show up, have a good time, and try not to say or do anything they wouldn't want to read about in the next issue of the company newsletter. But in smaller firms and the public-service sector, it's a different scenario. If your workplace falls into the latter categories, you know that holiday time brings a mixed blessing. It means that most, if not all, of the work of the annual gathering falls to you and your colleagues. But it also means that you have more say in how, when, and where you celebrate.

If you are involved in scheduling the annual party, ask the staff how they'd like to honor the holidays in the workplace by gathering everyone around the conference table or conducting a survey by e-mail.

For many people—especially those who might view the office party as a professional commitment more than a social

Responsible Drinking

If you'll be serving alcohol at your office party, it's important to make sure no one imbibes too much. Serve foods that are high in protein and carbohydrates, both of which slow the absorption of alcohol. Include plenty of nonalcoholic drinks (other than mixers) at the bar, and put away the liquor well before the party is over.

occasion—scheduling is crucial. Ask your coworkers whether they'd prefer to hold the gathering at lunchtime or after work, on a weeknight or a weekend. What might seem like great fun to people who live solo may be a logistical nightmare for working couples and single parents.

The timing within the season might be a problem for still other people. Depending on the size and the religious and ethnic diversity of your company, finding an evening that doesn't conflict with other

If anyone objects to seasonal symbols such as Christmas trees, omit them. No holiday is worth the expense of hurt feelings.

events—be they Kwanzaa or Hanukkah celebrations at home, Christmas pageants at church, or a spouse's office party—can be all but impossible. Your best bet may be simply to gather everyone's input and choose a date that works for the majority of the staff members.

Ask your cohorts whether they want to include spouses and significant others in the gathering. As in the case of scheduling, you might get a mixed response. Most likely, many employees will be delighted to have an evening out with their romantic partners. For some parents, though, a couples' party is simply one more occasion when they need to find (and pay) a babysitter. And it's a safe bet that at least a few single people will feel under pressure to produce a date for the evening, whether they want to invite someone or not.

The holidays wouldn't be the holidays if you didn't indulge a little. Work off those extra calories by getting more exercise.

To preserve office tranquillity before, during, and after the holiday period, urge everyone to be candid about their reactions to seasonal symbols. Especially in regard to Christmas, the secular and the religious have become so entwined over the centuries that in many cases there are no clear boundaries: What some people perceive to be a religious icon, such as a Christmas tree, is a secular trapping to others. And whenever office politics is involved, the best rule is that if anyone objects to something—whatever it is, and for whatever reason—omit it. No holiday is worth the expense of hurt feelings and a strained work environment.

Once you've established the broad outline of your celebration, get down to details. Toss out suggestions, ask for feedback, and don't hesitate to break long-standing traditions. For instance, maybe

you've always gone out to a restaurant for lunch. Or maybe you've staged an office potluck, with everyone bringing goodies ranging from chip dip to four-layer tortes. This year, ask coworkers how they'd feel about a catered buffet at the office (provided there's a budget for it), where they can mingle and chat more freely than they could seated at a restaurant table and for which no one will have to prepare yet another batch of holiday food.

Such an in-depth planning process might seem cumbersome at first, but it's worth all the effort you can give it. The more you can do to weed out traditions that complicate people's lives throughout the year-end holiday period—or at any other holiday time—the more smoothly your workplace is likely to function, and the better everyone will be able to relax and enjoy the celebration.

BRINGING it
all Home

---☀---

1 Celebrate Chinese New Year and other **national** holidays to honor your own heritage or to share good times with friends from other backgrounds. **2** Use **festivals** such as Mardi Gras and ceremonial processions such as Mexico's Las Posadas as themes for holiday parties. **3** Explore Christmas **traditions** of your ethnic heritage and incorporate them into your celebrations. **4** Enrich your Christmas celebrations by adopting (or adapting) appealing **customs** from other cultures. **5** Draw on Christmas decorations from Eastern countries such as India and Japan to add **variety** to your own decor. **6** Use Christmastime holidays such as Lucia Day and Saint Nicholas Day as opportunities to give **parties** before the stress of the season reaches its peak. **7** Tell your kids the story of the **real** Saint Nicholas to help ease their inevitable separation from Santa Claus. **8** Focus on Twelfth Night and the Feast of the Epiphany as times to encourage your children's **generosity.** Take them shopping for toys and books to give to needy children. ●

THE WORLD
LOVES A HOLIDAY

SHARING THE JOY OF ETHNIC AND
NATIONAL CELEBRATIONS

* —— * —— *

The speed of travel and communication as well as the growing global economy have made the world a melting pot, with immigrants arriving daily in every developed country. These newcomers bring their own traditions and festivities to their adopted homes, shaping them to fit local customs even as they enrich the celebrations of their new neighbors.

Whether you are curious about the customs of your friends and neighbors or you yearn to explore the traditions of your own ethnic heritage, adopting (or adapting) holiday customs from other countries can add meaning and joy to your holiday calendar. Such festivities needn't be elaborate: In fact, they can even simplify your celebrations by providing a theme for a spring or summer picnic or a focus for a Christmas gathering. However you choose to celebrate these holidays, you can add maximum fun for minimum fuss.

A GLOBEFUL OF CELEBRATIONS

---✳---

Taking part in the holidays of the world's many cultures can help you relive fond memories of foreign journeys or give you common festive ground with friends and relatives from other places.

Whatever your motivation, broadening your holiday repertoire can be a rewarding experience. This collection of round-the-world ideas can help get you started.

CHINESE NEW YEAR

Of all the Asian New Year celebrations, Chinese New Year is the one best known among non-Asians. It is also among the world's most exuberant holidays. According to the lunar calendar on which the traditional Asian year is based, New Year's

A colorful dragon *snakes through the streets at Chinese New Year to scare off evil spirits. The ball represents a pearl used to attract it.*

Day falls sometime between mid-January and mid-February. Though details of the celebration can vary from place to place, the festivities begin with a day or two of private family gatherings, then move on to roughly two weeks of parties in homes and social clubs and in the streets.

In Chinese homes, New Year's Eve and New Year's Day are observed as a time of reunion, thanksgiving, and remembrance of departed family and friends—and as a time of feasting. Food and flowers abound, all of them symbolic. In cities with large Chinese populations, public celebrations are colorful and noisy, with parades winding through the streets and firecrackers

exploding all around. The culmination comes on the fifteenth day of the celebration, with a parade of colorful floats and huge mythical creatures. Vibrantly colored, outsize papier-mâché lions prance along the parade route, paving the way for the star of the event: a magnificent dragon, usually made of opulent golden silk and often measuring over 100 feet (30m) long, which weaves its way through the streets in a classic reptilian dance.

This is an appealing holiday to observe, coming as it does at a time when winter has just about outstayed its welcome, at least in the north. And because it's an extended celebration, you're not tied down to a single day for a party, as you are for New Year's Eve on the Western calendar. If you don't live near a center of Asian-American culture such as San Francisco or New York, forget about being "correct" or "accurate" in your festivities—the object

Chinese New Year celebrations are colorful and noisy, with parades winding through the streets and firecrackers exploding everywhere.

here is to simplify your celebrations, not to complicate them. Rather, pick up a few ideas that engage your sense of fun, and carry on from there. (A full explanation of Chinese holiday symbolism would fill a book—and does, in fact, fill many. If the subject intrigues you, search under the heading "Festivals—China" or "China—Social life and customs" in your library's catalog, or visit an Asian bookstore.)

To Your Health, Chinese Style

No Chinese New Year celebration would be complete without *jiaozi* dumplings (also called Peking ravioli), said to ensure good health. You can buy them frozen (with pork, vegetable, or shrimp filling) in Asian markets. Simply boil or steam them, and serve with Chinese hot mustard or other dipping sauces.

For most Westerners, the best thing about Chinese New Year is its vitality and color. What could be more welcome at the dreary end of winter than a room decorated for a party in vibrant golds and reds—the traditional Chinese colors of wealth and good fortune? Flowers and blooming plants are important, too. Use them with abandon, as the Chinese do at festival time. Not only do they symbolize rebirth and new growth, but they also augur prosperity in the coming year. Red azaleas are propitious—and easy to find in any florist shop in February. Narcissi, peach blossoms, and camellias also carry good omens. In San Francisco's Chinatown, you'll see exquisite branches of reddish-pink flowering quince sold on every street corner. Elsewhere they won't be as easy to come by, but if you can get your hands on some quince branches, it's simple to force them to flower. Cut two- to three-foot stems when the buds have just begun to swell. Smash the cut ends of

CELEBRATE!

---✳---

I F YOU'D LIKE TO EXPLORE more holiday traditions of other cultures, celebrate these simple but meaningful days from around the world. They can help you bridge the festivity gap between your own holidays— and remind you that someone, somewhere is always celebrating.

WOMEN'S DAY
Russia, March 8

International Women's Day is celebrated around the world, but nowhere more fervently than in Russia, where it began in 1910. Here men and children shower the women in their lives—their wives, mothers, sisters, girlfriends, teachers, and friends—with gifts and praise.

You can celebrate Women's Day by giving flowers or small gifts to all the women in your life, and spending some time talking with your kids about famous women or those who made a difference in your own life.

CHILDREN'S DAY
Japan, May 5

The Japanese set aside a day to pray for the health and happiness of the country's children. Adults give them gifts and special treats such as sweet rice dumplings. People string paper carp (representing strength) from poles; they flap in the wind as if they were swimming.

If your kids think it's unfair that there isn't a Children's Day when there's a Father's Day and a Mother's Day, why not indulge them by giving them their own day? Take time on the weekend nearest May 5 and spend a whole day doing what your kids want to do: Visit the zoo, ride bikes to the park and have a picnic, or take them roller-skating. Prepare their favorite meals and give them small gifts.

DRAGON BOAT FESTIVAL
China, June

The exact date of the festival depends on the Chinese lunar calendar, but it normally falls in June. The festival originated when the poet Qu Yuan fell into a river in 277 B.C. and drowned. Onlookers tried to distract fish from eating his body by feeding them rice dumplings. Today, some Chinese communities mark the date by staging boat races and eating rice dumplings.

You can honor the poet on a weekend in June by throwing a party at a nearby lake or reservoir and renting paddleboats or rowboats for racing. Serve Chinese fare, especially dim sum, and read translations of the poet's work.

MIDSUMMER FESTIVAL
Scandinavia, June 20 to 26

In late June in Scandinavia, the sun barely dips below the horizon, and Scandinavians mark the yearly event as they have since pre-Christian times. Many travel to their summer homes in the country, where they bedeck themselves with flowers and stay awake until morning, dancing, eating, and drinking.

If you want to celebrate midsummer, hold an evening barbecue and watch the sky as the stars come out. Or throw a late-night garden party and serve Nordic fare such as chilled vodka, grilled salmon, new potatoes with dill, and strawberries with cream.

DÍAS DE LOS MUERTOS
Mexico, November 1 and 2

Mexicans honor their ancestors in these annual "Days of the Dead." The first day, a group winds through the streets carrying a coffin with someone playing a corpse. People then head to the cemetery to picnic on the graves of deceased relatives. They spend the night in the cemetery and clean and decorate the graves the next day.

This festivity is a way to celebrate and honor your own departed relatives: Serve food they liked and remember them with stories and photographs. Serve Mexican treats such as coconut candy and skeleton cookies.

the stems with a hammer, then place them in water in a cool (60–70°F [16–21°C]), bright room and change the water every few days. In about two weeks, you'll have glorious quince blossoms.

Food for a Chinese New Year celebration can be as simple or as complex as you choose to make it. Like flowering plants, virtually every item on a Chinese menu is filled with symbolism that applies to any season. Favorites for the New Year include a chicken dumpling soup called "Broth of Prosperity" and semitransparent strands of bean vermicelli called "Silver Threads of Longevity." But, according to custom, the surest way to bring good luck during the coming year is to serve a whole, fresh fish—head and tail included. Check your local bookstore or Chinese New Year sites on the Internet for collections of recipes, symbolism of popular foods, and tips on cooking Asian style. In areas with large

At a Mardi Gras parade, *crowds clamor for "throws"—coins, beads, and trinkets that are tossed from floats by costumed riders.*

and urge everyone to help drive away the evil spirits of the past year. Get a book on Chinese astrology, which is based on

Favorite foods for Chinese New Year include a soup called "Broth of Prosperity" and noodles called "Silver Threads of Longevity."

Asian populations, local newspapers may also carry delicious Chinese New Year recipes around the holiday time.

Some Chinese restaurants are closed on Chinese New Year's Eve and New Year's Day. But if you find a good one that will be open, you can reserve banquet tables and order a New Year's menu in advance. Or simply call and ask the chefs to prepare a New Year's meal that you can pick up. Take it home and serve it on Oriental dishes on a table decked out in red and gold. After dinner, hand out noisemakers

the year of a person's birth rather than on the month, day, and hour, and have fun telling your guests' fortunes.

MARDI GRAS

Everyone knows about Mardi Gras, but outside the Latin countries and a handful of cities in the southern United States— preeminently New Orleans—few people do much to celebrate it. For Christians, it's the last day before the start of Lent, a time of fasting and repentance that culminates with Easter. The name—which in

French means "Fat Tuesday"—is given to this day because it's traditionally the time to use up all the butter, eggs, and fat before giving them up for the next 40 days.

Where it's celebrated on a grand scale, Mardi Gras is the culmination of a boisterous and decidedly nonreligious season called Carnival, which begins with parties on Twelfth Night and gathers momentum as it nears Fat Tuesday. By the final week of this marathon celebration, the merriment has outgrown living rooms and private clubs and spilled out into the streets in parades and raucous festivals.

There could be few better excuses for a party—and few more buoyant themes to carry out. Decorate in the tongue-in-cheek style of a Mardi Gras parade, with colorful streamers and a multitude of plastic beads and fake coins strewn about to imitate the ones tossed from parade floats. Hand out noisemakers and standard New Orleans drinks like hurricanes and Ramos gin fizzes (you'll find recipes in any basic cocktail book). Serve Cajun food, such as blackened fish (red snapper and ocean perch are both good choices) or red beans and rice. Purchase a pecan pie or pralines for dessert, and give it all a musical backdrop of classic New Orleans jazz.

MAY DAY

In pre-Christian western Europe, this celebration, known as Beltane, hailed the coming of sunlight and fertility. The warmth of spring had at last defeated the deathlike cold of winter, and the world was a living panorama of verdant fields, sweet-smelling flowers, and newborn animals. The change was enough to make even the most rational person downright giddy, and it usually did. The accompanying festivities, while not always suitable for family entertainment, have formed the basis of a number of charming holiday traditions.

The maypole is one symbol of Beltane. It gained popularity in England during the Middle Ages, then traveled across the Atlantic to the colonies in the 1600's. Dancing around the maypole was a favorite May Day treat for children, and the custom still lingers among adults who practice Morris dancing. The maypole was simply a post stuck in the ground—the taller the better—with long, colorful ribbons attached at the top and streaming down to ground level. Children (or anyone else who was so

SIMPLY PUT...

MARDI GRAS TERMS

masker • A masked and costumed rider on a parade float, or any other reveler who dresses in costume for the festivities of Mardi Gras.

Rex • The ceremonial king of Carnival, who with his queen presides over events with a court of maids, dukes, and assorted other "royalty."

throws • Cheap trinkets that are tossed into the exultant crowd from passing parade floats. They include strands of plastic beads and pearls, small plastic toys, and commemorative coins called doubloons.

Let kids celebrate spring by weaving ribbons around a maypole.

inclined) would hold on to the streamers' ends and execute a merry dance around the pole, weaving a colorful braid of ribbons in the process. Dancing in the opposite direction made the weaving come undone. Though teenagers may disdain such folly, small children and toddlers love it. Why not make the maypole the centerpiece of an easy welcome-to-spring party for everyone in your neighborhood?

You could also include another children's custom that is ripe for revival: making May baskets. As recently as the 1940's and 1950's in some communities, youngsters practiced this reverse version of trick-or-treat. They made colorful paper baskets, filled them with flowers and candy, and left them at friends' doors. According to the May Day rules, you hung the basket by its handle on the doorknob, rang the bell,

and ran. You could honor this tradition—and brighten someone's day—by encouraging your kids to make a few May baskets to take to nursing homes or convalescent hospitals, or as presents for older neighbors, grandparents, and great-aunts and great-uncles, who perhaps made May baskets themselves when they were small.

CINCO DE MAYO

Though Cinco de Mayo is a Mexican holiday, it gets far more attention in the United States than it does south of the border. Contrary to popular misinformation, it does not mark the date of Mexican independence. Rather, it commemorates the Battle of Puebla, in which, on May 5, 1862, Mexican soldiers defeated a much larger, better-equipped French force that was attempting to take over the country.

SIMPLE SOLUTIONS

HOLIDAY RESEARCH

FINDING OUT MORE about another culture's holidays can be a
challenge if you don't live near a community of immigrants and
their descendants. Here are some approaches to learning more
about other nations' holidays and customs.

Simple Consult books and articles. Ask your librarian for help in finding books
about international holidays, or search a newspaper index for articles
from cities with diverse ethnic groups.

Simpler Search the Web. The Internet's World Wide Web is a treasure trove of
information about holidays near and far. There you'll find histories, mail-
order sources, and even authentic holiday music.

Simplest Ask someone. Call a nearby university and speak to someone in the language department, ask the owner of a local ethnic restaurant, or chat
with coworkers who come from other countries.

(Mexico had been a sovereign nation for quite some time by then.) The French won later battles and went on to rule Mexico for the next five years, but the Battle of Puebla was a point of pride for Mexicans because they defeated such a well-trained army. This pride also led to a nationalistic

You can honor Cinco de Mayo by throwing a fiesta. Put out the fixings for make-it-yourself burritos, and dance to mariachi music.

movement that forced the end of European domination. Today, Cinco de Mayo is celebrated mainly in Mexican-American culture—and, like Saint Patrick's Day, it makes a great excuse for a party.

You can honor the memory of Mexico's victory by throwing a simple fiesta. Barbecue steak or fish, put out fixings for

make-it-yourself burritos, and serve lots of Mexican beer. Then dance off all those calories to the buoyant strains of mariachi music—either live or on CD or tape.

If these simple ideas for celebrating the holidays of other cultures have piqued your curiosity, check out libraries, the Internet, and your local bookstore for ideas and inspiration that can add sparkle to the holidays you currently observe—and show you some exciting new occasions you can celebrate easily and inexpensively.

For children, delving into the rituals of their own ethnic heritage and those of others is not only fun in its own right, but it can also give them a better understanding and appreciation of different cultures.

As the world grows more tightly knit, understanding its various celebrations— and observing them in simple and meaningful ways—can help us all feel more a part of the global community.

CHRISTMAS AROUND THE WORLD

---*---

THROUGHOUT THE WORLD, NO HOLIDAY IS AS WIDELY CELEBRATED AS CHRIST-
MAS. ITS MAGIC IS SUCH THAT IT HAS ASSUMED STATURE EVEN IN CHINA,
JAPAN, AND INDIA, WHERE CHRISTIANITY IS NOT THE PRIMARY FAITH.

Christmas celebrations around the world range from the very secular—as in Japan, Singapore, and Hong Kong—to the highly religious—as in Italy and all the Spanish-speaking countries. But regardless of their focus, all these cultures have Christmas foods, decorations, and activities you can easily adopt or adapt to make your own celebrations more enjoyable.

Even something as simple as a novel decorating idea can add a cosmopolitan sparkle to your holiday. In India, where generations of British colonists left behind a Christmas legacy, people light small clay oil lamps and line them up along the tops of roofs and walls, where they shine amid the scarlet bracts of poinsettias —which grow to tree size in the tropical climate. Inexpensive pottery lamps are easy to find in import stores and through houseware catalogs. Place them along your sidewalk or driveway, or arrange lamps and poinsettias on your table as a centerpiece for a dinner party with an Indian menu.

Though Christianity is by no means a majority religion in Japan, the Japanese people have enthusiastically adopted the

Sweden's Lucia Day *blends Christian and pagan traditions. Girls dress as the martyred Saint Lucia and bear candles to herald the return of light after the winter solstice.*

Hanging up a piñata is an easy way to add fun to a Christmas fiesta.

concepts of peace and generosity that the Christmas season epitomizes. The Christmas tree is a major focal point of the celebration, and it's trimmed to the hilt with toys and dolls, wind chimes, paper fans, and origami ornaments.

The origami pieces are made from colorful paper squares that are folded into animal and geometric shapes. You can buy premade origami ornaments at museum shops and some craft fairs, or make your own with special origami paper or small sheets of colored paper. Packaged assortments are available at craft shops and art-supply stores, where you can find books describing the technique.

LAS POSADAS

One of the more charming Christmas celebrations is Las Posadas, which is popular in Mexico and parts of the southwestern United States. (*Posada* is Spanish for lodging or inn.) There are many variations, but Las Posadas usually begins as a procession in each village or neighborhood on December 16 and continues every night until Christmas Eve. In essence, it is a traveling play with nine nightly performances—and a neighborhood fiesta for all ages. The stars are a small girl dressed as Mary and a small boy representing Joseph, who travel from house to house, reenacting the couple's search for lodging in Bethlehem. They're accompanied by other children carrying candles and dressed as angels, shepherds, shepherdesses, and the Three Wise Men, and by their parents, who act as a traveling audience. At each house, "Mary" and "Joseph" sing a song requesting shelter, and each time the residents (playing the parts of innkeepers) turn them away, saying, "There's no room at the inn." When the children have called at all the houses along the predetermined route, the procession disbands, only to travel the same route on the following evening.

Finally, on Christmas Eve, the procession reaches its climax: "Mary" and "Joseph" arrive at the last house on the route and are told that though there is no room at the inn, they are welcome to sleep in the stable. Of course, there is no real stable and nobody intends to sleep; instead, everyone goes inside for a fiesta.

Even if you approach it as pure entertainment rather than as religious reenactment, Las Posadas can be a lot of fun for kids—and for their parents—even in the snowy north. On Christmas Eve, let the kids parade up and down the block—or through the hallways of your apartment building—knocking at each door where the inhabitants expect them.

a suitor revealed her identity as a Christian when she spurned him, and Roman officials set out to torture and kill her. Legend has it that the Romans plucked out her eyes, but God restored her sight.

Lucia's legend spread quickly throughout Europe. In some stories, she is said to have become a star in the sky, descending on occasion to bring food to people in the midst of famine. Lucia's head is always encircled by a halo of lights (in fact, she is often referred to as the "Queen of Light," and indeed her name *Lucia* derives from the Latin word for light).

The people of the winter-dark Scandinavian countries, particularly Sweden, were understandably drawn to Lucia and

On Lucia Day the eldest daughter, wearing a long white dress and a crown of greens and candles, wakens the family and brings them breakfast.

As the group leaves each house or apartment, the residents trail along—and when everyone reaches your place, they all come in for a fiesta. Have a piñata for the children to break (they're available at Mexican markets and party-supply stores). Serve a feast of tamales, chicken mole, enchiladas, and a salad made of fruit and greens. Provide cinnamon-spiked hot chocolate for the children and margaritas or imported Mexican beer for the grown-ups.

LUCIA DAY

December 13 is one of the most important dates of Sweden's Christmas season. The date honors Lucia, a Christian who lived in ancient Rome during the reign of an anti-Christian emperor. As her story goes,

her halo of lights. There, Lucia Day (or *Lussidagen,* as it is referred to in Swedish) is a school holiday—with parades, games, and caroling in the streets—but the most significant part of the celebration revolves around breakfast. Traditionally, the eldest daughter of the household, wearing a long white dress with a scarlet sash and a crown of greens set with lighted candles (originally real, now often battery-powered for safety reasons), wakens the rest of the family and brings them coffee, ginger-flavored cookies known as *pepparkakor,* and large saffron-infused rolls called *lussekattor.*

Even if your daughter isn't up to all that baking, Lucia Day is a wonderful occasion to know about, since entertaining in mid-December can ease the social crunch that tends to come as Christmas draws closer. For the sake of convenience and a large, joyful turnout, hold your event on the weekend that's closest to the feast day. And, in honor of Lucia's reputation for delivering sustenance to Christians in hiding, have all of your guests bring cans of food for a local charity.

Instead of offering ginger cookies and *lussekattor*, you can serve coffee cake and other party treats of your choice. But the authentic goodies are all simple to make; you can find recipes and instructions in most Scandinavian and many other holiday baking books. You can also buy everything prebaked in many import shops. If your kids want to take part in the festivities, check those same import shops for battery-powered versions of Lucia's headdress. Or adapt the crown for use as a

decoration: On a table or sideboard, secure seven white tapers in candleholders and place them in a circle. Weave some evergreen boughs between and around the candles to form a wreath. Light the candles, and you'll have a traditional version of the Lucia crown that will add to your holiday decor for a week or longer.

SAINT NICHOLAS DAY

One of the most cherished Christmas traditions is the legend of a mythical character who travels the world one night of the year, leaving presents for sleeping children. The dates of this journey vary: In some cultures, the gift giver makes an appearance on the night of December 5, in others December 24, in still others January 5. In each case, children awake to find treasures the following morning.

Though celebrated in many different ways,
Christmas is familiar around the world.

The identity of this giver differs with the culture—it's an old woman in Italy and Russia, a baby camel in Syria, a gnome in Sweden. In several countries, the Three Wise Men deliver the gifts; in others it's the Christ Child himself. By far, though, the busiest gift giver at Christmastime is the figure called Saint Nicholas, who is also known as Santa Claus in the United States and English-speaking Canada, Père Noël in French-speaking countries, Father Christmas in Great Britain, Sinterklaas in Holland, Santa Kurohsu in Japan, and Dun Che Lao Ren in China.

Mythology notwithstanding, Saint Nicholas was a real person—a fourth-century bishop of the city of Myra, in what is now Turkey. He was known in his time for his great fondness for children, and today

Saint Nicholas Day is an excellent occasion for a children's party— especially since it takes place before the last-minute rush.

the good bishop is best remembered for one simple act of human kindness. According to the story, three impoverished sisters were on the brink of being forced into prostitution because they lacked the dowry necessary for marriage. Nicholas, a quiet man who preferred to keep his good deeds to himself, heard of their plight and, under cover of darkness, tossed three bags of gold into the girls' home, saving them from an unpleasant fate.

After his death, Nicholas went on to become the patron saint of children, and

Cookies in the Nick of Time

Use a Saint Nicholas Day party as an excuse to get your holiday baking off to an early start. Have the kids help you bake the gingery speculaas cookies that are traditionally associated with Saint Nick (check in holiday baking books). Make enough so you can store some in the freezer to pull out as the season unfolds.

each year on the eve of December 6, his Christian feast day, Saint Nicholas was said to ride his horse throughout much of Europe. Dressed in his bishop's robe and miter, he'd leave presents for all youngsters who had been nice rather than naughty during the year. Dutch immigrants carried Saint Nicholas—or Sinterklaas, as they called him—to America, where the name eventually became anglicized to Santa Claus. In most countries the night of his yearly journey gradually moved to December 24 to coincide with Christmas.

Back in Holland, though—as well as in Germany, Switzerland, Luxembourg, and parts of France—Saint Nick continues to deliver presents on the night of December 5. Christmas Day is reserved for quiet family gatherings and for the spiritual celebration of the birth of Christ.

Although moving gift giving to December 6 is probably impractical if your children are used to opening presents on

Coming Down From the Holidays

De-stress post-holiday cleanup by holding a family "undecorating" party on Twelfth Night or on the Feast of the Epiphany, which follows the next day. Use the time to take down the tree at a leisurely pace and to carefully sort through and store your decorations so you know where to find them next year.

Christmas morning, Saint Nicholas Day is an excellent occasion for a children's party —especially as it falls early in the season before the rush sets in. And telling your kids the story of the real Saint Nicholas can help ease their transition from belief in a magical Santa Claus to a more realistic vision of the Christmas spirit.

TWELFTH NIGHT

In many places, Santa's equivalent arrives not in December but on Twelfth Night, January 5, so that children open their gifts on the sixth. Also called the Feast of the Epiphany or El Día de los Reyes, January 6 is the day the Three Magi are said to have arrived at the manger in Bethlehem. In Spanish-speaking countries this same trio delivers gifts to children, who leave their shoes outside the door, filled with grain for the Wise Men's camels. In Italy on the night of January 5, an old woman called La Befana fills the children's stockings.

If you're concerned about the glut of gifts your kids receive at Christmas, consider using the Feast of the Epiphany—and the ancient tradition of giving that it represents—as a chance to encourage your family's generosity. Take them shopping for toys and books to give to needy children. To further commemorate the day, let the kids decorate a frosted king cake. This traditional dessert is a cake decorated to look like a crown in honor of the Three Kings. A white-frosted bundt cake, either homemade or store-bought, makes a good base. Turn the kids loose in decorating the cake to resemble a king's crown. They can use colored icing, cookies to make the scalloped points, and "jewels" in the form of gumdrops, jelly beans, cinnamon imperials, or colored sugar sprinkles.

Twelfth Night and the Feast of the Epiphany are times to celebrate the end of the Christmas season and reflect on its meaning.

Before you cut the "crown," have a simple, leisurely dinner. This is the ideal time to reflect on the year and the holiday season that have just passed. Discuss what each of you enjoyed most, what you found most meaningful, and what you might like to do next year. Don't view it as a planning session; rather, use the time as a chance to learn what each member of your family saw as significant about the Christmas season and the way that your family celebrated it. You might be surprised to hear some of their impressions.

CHECKLISTS
AND RESOURCES

INFORMATION FOR HOLIDAY REVELERS

* —— * —— *

With so much going on during the holiday season, it's easy to get bogged down in all the details. The lists in this chapter will help you stay organized so you have more time for joyful celebration with friends and family. Photocopy the pages to use again and again through years of holidays.

You'll find lists to help you shop for gifts, plan holiday parties, and clean up after the season is over so everything is easy to find next year. Other lists are meant to spark your own creativity, including gift ideas for various categories of recipients and activities to enjoy when the family gets together. For those evenings when you're sitting around at the ski lodge or snowed in at Grandma's, there are lists of holiday movies and literature that will delight both kids and adults.

Finally, at the end of the chapter you'll find names of publications, suppliers, and organizations for practical help and creative inspiration in all your holiday planning.

BEST HOLIDAY FILMS

MOVIES FOR FAMILIES TO WATCH TOGETHER

———— ✳ ————

CHRISTMAS IS A FAVORITE TOPIC FOR FILMMAKERS, WHO PRODUCE A HOLIDAY MOVIE ALMOST EVERY YEAR. MANY OF THEM HAVE BECOME CLASSICS. THE FOLLOWING MOVIES WILL DELIGHT EVERYONE IN THE FAMILY.

Babes in Toyland
Directed by Jack Donohue, 1961
Starring Annette Funicello and
Ray Bolger

The Bishop's Wife
Directed by Henry Koster, 1947
Starring Cary Grant, Loretta Young,
and David Niven

A Charlie Brown Christmas
Directed by Bill Melendez, 1965
Animated

A Christmas Carol
Directed by Brian Desmond-Hurst, 1951
Starring Alastair Sim

Christmas in Connecticut
Directed by Peter Godfrey, 1945
Starring Barbara Stanwyck, Dennis
Morgan, and Sydney Greenstreet

A Christmas Story
Directed by Bob Clark, 1983
Starring Peter Billingsley, Darren
McGavin, and Melinda Dillon

Holiday Inn
Directed by Mark Sandrich, 1942
Starring Bing Crosby and Fred Astaire

How the Grinch Stole Christmas
Directed by Chuck Jones, 1966
Narrated by Boris Karloff

It's a Wonderful Life
Directed by Frank Capra, 1946
Starring James Stewart and
Donna Reed

Miracle on 34th Street
Directed by George Seaton, 1947
Starring Maureen O'Hara and
John Payne

The Muppet Christmas Carol
Directed by Brian Henson, 1992
With the voice of Michael Caine

The Nutcracker
Directed by Tony Charmoli, 1977
Starring Mikhail Baryshnikov

Scrooge
Directed by Ronald Neame, 1970
Starring Albert Finney, Alec Guinness,
and Edith Evans

White Christmas
Directed by Michael Curtiz, 1954
Starring Bing Crosby, Danny Kaye,
and Rosemary Clooney

CLASSIC HOLIDAY LITERATURE

GOOD READING FOR THE CHRISTMAS SEASON

———————— ✳ ————————

LITERATURE WITH A CHRISTMAS THEME ABOUNDS. THE FOLLOWING WILL ENTERTAIN BOTH CHILDREN AND ADULTS—READ THEM SILENTLY OR ALOUD, OR LISTEN TO RECORDED VERSIONS WHILE YOU'RE TRAVELING.

BOOKS

Amahl and the Night Visitors
Based on opera by
Gian Carlo Menotti

A Child's Christmas in Wales
Dylan Thomas

A Christmas Carol
Charles Dickens

The Father Christmas Letters
J. R. R. Tolkien

The Fir Tree
Hans Christian Andersen

The Little Match Girl
Hans Christian Andersen

The Story of the Other Wise Man
Henry Van Dyke

SHORT STORIES

"The Adventure of the Blue Carbuncle"
Sir Arthur Conan Doyle

"The Gift of the Magi"
O. Henry

"A Letter From Santa Claus"
Mark Twain

"The Seven Poor Travelers"
Charles Dickens

POEMS

"A Christmas Carol"
Christina Rossetti

"The Christmas Dinner"
Washington Irving

"Christmas Trees"
Robert Frost

MISCELLANEOUS

"Bird of Dawning"
Hamlet, act 1, scene 1
William Shakespeare

The Gospel According
to Matthew
King James Version

Chapter 2, "A Merry Christmas"
from *Little Women*
Louisa May Alcott

"Yes, Virginia, There
Is a Santa Claus"
Francis P. Church
column in *New York Sun*
September 21, 1897

FAMILY ACTIVITIES

HOLIDAY FUN FOR KIDS AND ADULTS

———— ✳ ————

S O YOU'RE ALL TOGETHER AT LAST—NOW WHAT? WHETHER YOU'RE TRYING TO KEEP LITTLE ONES OCCUPIED OR YOU'RE LOOKING FOR ACTIVITIES TO HELP RENEW FAMILY TIES, THIS LIST CAN MAKE FAMILY VISITS MORE ENJOYABLE.

LOCAL OUTINGS

◆ Go Christmas caroling in your neighborhood

◆ Take everyone tobogganing or to a skating rink

◆ Take a tour of neighborhood light decorations

EVENTS

◆ Attend the outdoor tree-lighting ceremony for your town

◆ Attend a holiday concert or ballet performance

◆ Attend First Night or Revels celebrations (see page 143)

◆ Participate in local "fun runs"

HELPING OTHERS

◆ Visit a local nursing home or hospital

◆ Volunteer at a nearby shelter or soup kitchen

◆ Join a church fund-raiser

AT HOME TOGETHER

◆ Play board games such as Monopoly, Scrabble, and Trivial Pursuit

◆ Get out a deck of cards and start a game of hearts—or slapjack for the little ones

◆ Set up a card table and collaborate on a giant jigsaw puzzle

◆ Bake and decorate cookies and gingerbread houses

Schedule activities that will keep the gathering lively.

GIFT PLANNING GUIDE

PERSONAL PROFILES TO HELP YOU SHOP

Finding the perfect gifts for friends and relatives is easier when you know about the recipients' interests and needs. Copy this list as needed and fill in information to take along when you shop.

Name _____
Clothing size _____
_____
Hobbies and interests _____
_____
Last year's gift _____
Gift ideas for this year _____
_____
_____

Name _____
Clothing size _____
_____
Hobbies and interests _____
_____
Last year's gift _____
Gift ideas for this year _____
_____
_____

Name _____
Clothing size _____
_____
Hobbies and interests _____
_____
Last year's gift _____
Gift ideas for this year _____
_____
_____

Name _____
Clothing size _____
_____
Hobbies and interests _____
_____
Last year's gift _____
Gift ideas for this year _____
_____
_____

Name _____
Clothing size _____
_____
Hobbies and interests _____
_____
Last year's gift _____
Gift ideas for this year _____
_____
_____

Name _____
Clothing size _____
_____
Hobbies and interests _____
_____
Last year's gift _____
Gift ideas for this year _____
_____
_____

SIMPLE GIFTS

IDEAS FOR EVERYONE ON YOUR LIST

———— ✳ ————

Gift giving should be an act of joy, but crowded malls, long wish lists, and too many choices can turn it into an ordeal. Use this list to make shopping easier by honing down your choices.

CHILDREN UNDER 5 YEARS
- ☐ Books
- ☐ Classic videos
- ☐ Clothing for dress-up
- ☐ Day at the zoo, botanical garden, or children's museum
- ☐ Easy puzzles
- ☐ Sandbox and bathtub toys
- ☐ Skating or skiing lessons
- ☐ Sticker collections
- ☐ Stuffed toys

CHILDREN 5 TO 12 YEARS
- ☐ Art supplies
- ☐ Bird feeder and child's bird book
- ☐ Board games and puzzles
- ☐ Books and comics
- ☐ Child-size garden tools
- ☐ Children's magazine subscription
- ☐ Clothing for impromptu plays
- ☐ Day at the zoo, botanical garden, or children's museum
- ☐ Disposable camera and photo album
- ☐ Learn-to-cook kit
- ☐ Magic tricks kit
- ☐ Modeling clay
- ☐ Models and kits
- ☐ Music, dance, or art lessons
- ☐ Puppet theater

- ☐ Sports equipment
- ☐ Sticker books
- ☐ Tickets to sporting events (accompanied by adult of choice)
- ☐ Videos

TEENAGERS
- ☐ Art, music, or cooking lessons
- ☐ Arts and crafts supplies
- ☐ Books
- ☐ Cartoon collections
- ☐ Gift certificates to a music store
- ☐ Magazine subscriptions
- ☐ Movie tickets
- ☐ Tickets to concerts or sporting events
- ☐ Videos

PARENTS
- ☐ Babysitting IOU
- ☐ Books
- ☐ Certificates for favorite stores
- ☐ Day at a spa
- ☐ Garden tools
- ☐ Gift certificate for lunch or dinner
- ☐ Gourmet food collections
- ☐ Housecleaning service
- ☐ Magazine subscriptions
- ☐ Monthly flower arrangements
- ☐ Monthly gourmet food shipments

- [ ] Monthly lunch or dinner date
- [ ] Museum membership
- [ ] Tickets to concerts or sporting events
- [ ] Wine

GRANDPARENTS

- [ ] Art, music, or language lessons
- [ ] Books
- [ ] Certificates for favorite stores
- [ ] Gourmet food collections
- [ ] Housecleaning service
- [ ] Lunch or dinner certificates
- [ ] Magazine subscriptions
- [ ] Monthly flower arrangements
- [ ] Monthly lunch or dinner date
- [ ] Museum membership
- [ ] Prepaid phone card
- [ ] Tickets to concerts or sporting events
- [ ] Wine
- [ ] Yard maintenance service

FRIENDS AND FAMILY

- [ ] Blooming plants
- [ ] Books
- [ ] Car safety kit (flares, flashlights, etc.)
- [ ] Certificates for favorite stores
- [ ] Classes and workshops
- [ ] Gourmet food collections
- [ ] Magazine subscriptions
- [ ] Museum memberships
- [ ] Personal tool kits
- [ ] Wine

COWORKERS

- [ ] Coffee mugs and gourmet coffee beans
- [ ] Decorative pencil cups, paperweights, and storage boxes

- [ ] Gift certificates to specialty shops
- [ ] Golf balls or other sports accessories
- [ ] Gourmet food gifts
- [ ] Restaurant certificates
- [ ] Wine

FAMILY GIFTS

- [ ] Badminton, croquet, or other outdoor game set
- [ ] Bread-making machine
- [ ] Classic board games
- [ ] Family museum membership
- [ ] Family zoo or botanical garden membership
- [ ] Ice-cream maker
- [ ] Playing cards and book of card games
- [ ] Tickets to concerts or sporting events

HANUKKAH GIFTS

- [ ] Biographies of historical figures
- [ ] Books on Jewish history
- [ ] Chocolate gelt
- [ ] Dreidels
- [ ] Family photo albums
- [ ] Homemade foods
- [ ] Menorahs
- [ ] Stationery and cards

KWANZAA GIFTS

- [ ] Art classes
- [ ] Art supplies
- [ ] Biographies of historical figures
- [ ] Books on African heritage
- [ ] Educational games
- [ ] Handmade gifts from wood or straw
- [ ] Museum memberships
- [ ] Science classes

PARTY PLANNING CHECKLIST

A TO-DO LIST FOR HOLIDAY GATHERINGS

———— ✳ ————

ADVANCE PLANNING IS ESPECIALLY CRUCIAL DURING THE HOLIDAY SEASON, WHEN EVERYONE FROM CLEANERS TO CATERERS IS IN HIGH DEMAND. USE THIS LIST TO HELP YOU PREPARE; SEE PAGE 106 FOR TIME GUIDELINES.

INITIAL DECISIONS

- ☐ Set the date, time, and location
- ☐ Decide on a theme
- ☐ Set a budget
- ☐ Compile the guest list
- ☐ Set the menu
- ☐ Decide on the entertainment
- ☐ Decide on the party activity (if any)

PLANNING

- ☐ Send invitations
- ☐ Hire any professional help
- ☐ Ask for volunteers
- ☐ Check equipment and supplies
- ☐ Finalize the menu and cooking schedule
- ☐ Make arrangements for kids and pets
- ☐ Plan seating

SHOPPING

- ☐ Shop for nonperishable foods and supplies
- ☐ Order food from vendors
- ☐ Order flowers and centerpieces
- ☐ Purchase perishable foods
- ☐ Pick up ice and other last-minute items

COOKING

- ☐ Prepare foods that can be frozen
- ☐ Assign potluck dishes (if any)

- ☐ Prepare and freeze make-ahead dishes
- ☐ Thaw premade frozen dishes
- ☐ Cut up salad ingredients
- ☐ Prepare last-minute dishes

SETTING UP

- ☐ Clean the house
- ☐ Wash china and glassware
- ☐ Polish silver pieces
- ☐ Wash and iron linens
- ☐ Assemble music tapes and CDs
- ☐ Clear space for the caterer
- ☐ Clear space for coats
- ☐ Pick up rented or borrowed items
- ☐ Arrange flowers and decorations
- ☐ Chill beverages
- ☐ Set up the bar
- ☐ Set up buffet tables
- ☐ Set out dishes, glassware, and cutlery
- ☐ Set out dips and finger foods
- ☐ Start the fire and light candles

FINISHING UP

- ☐ Put away or discard leftovers
- ☐ Wash and put away serving ware
- ☐ Clean house, launder linens
- ☐ Return rented, borrowed, or forgotten items
- ☐ Send thank-you notes to volunteers

AFTER-CHRISTMAS CLEANUP

GETTING READY THIS YEAR FOR NEXT YEAR

———— ✳ ————

I F THE IDEA OF TAKING DOWN THE CHRISTMAS TREE FILLS YOU WITH MELAN-
CHOLY, SIMPLY THINK OF THE END AS A BEGINNING. EVERY END-OF-SEASON
TASK YOU TAKE CARE OF NOW WILL BE ONE LESS TO TACKLE NEXT YEAR.

SUPPLIES TO ASSEMBLE

☐ Bubble wrap or other padding

☐ Marking pens

☐ Spindles or spools

☐ Strong tape

☐ Storage boxes in a range of sizes

THE TREE

☐ Strip the tree of ornaments and tinsel

☐ Replace any burned-out lightbulbs

☐ Wrap light strands on spindles

☐ Weed out unwanted ornaments

☐ Repair broken ornaments

☐ Wrap fragile ornaments in bubble wrap

☐ Wrap tinsel and garlands on spindles

☐ Check tree for forgotten ornaments

☐ Move tree outdoors for pickup

☐ Mulch tree or arrange for pickup

INDOOR DECORATIONS

☐ Take down wreaths and garlands

☐ Weed out unwanted decorations

☐ Repair or replace damaged items

☐ Toss partially burned candles

OUTDOOR DECORATIONS

☐ Replace any burned-out bulbs

☐ Wrap light strands on spindles

☐ Repair or replace damaged items

SERVING WARE AND LINENS

☐ Wash all dishes and glassware

☐ Polish silver; wrap in antitarnish cloth

☐ Replace any broken or missing items

☐ Clean and iron linens

BEFORE STORING

☐ Find a safe, dry storage place

☐ Label boxes clearly

☐ Seal boxes against dust and insects

PREPARING FOR NEXT YEAR

☐ Inventory what you have

☐ Note what you still need

☐ Assess what worked and what didn't

☐ Shop at after-holiday sales

Store holiday trappings where Santa
will find them easily next year.

Looking for additional details and guidance? Consult the publications, retail sources, and organizations listed here to help you with everything from gift giving and cooking to volunteering with charitable organizations.

PUBLICATIONS

Christmastime
By Sandra Boynton
(Workman Publishing, 1987)
Humorous look at the celebrations of the season.

**Christmas With
Martha Stewart Living**
By Martha Stewart and the
editors of *Martha Stewart Living*
(Clarkson Potter, 1997)
The best crafts, entertaining, and decorating ideas for the holiday season from Martha Stewart Living *magazine.*

**A Continual Feast: A Cookbook
to Celebrate the Joys of Family
and Faith Throughout the
Christian Year**
By Evelyn Birge Vitz
(Ignatius Press, 1991)
Recipes, menus, and background information for a year of Christian holidays.

**Family Traditions: Celebrations
for Holidays and Everyday**
By Elizabeth Berg
(Reader's Digest, 1994)
Suggestions for family celebrations throughout the year.

Gifts From the Herb Garden
By Emelie Tolley and Chris Mead
(Clarkson Potter, 1991)
Year-round gifts crafted from fresh and dried herbs.

Gifts That Make a Difference
By Ellen Berry
(Foxglove Publishing, 1992)
Profiles of 165 nonprofit organizations, with listings of the merchandise that supports their causes.

**Gifts That Save the Animals:
1001 Great Gifts Sold by
Nonprofits That Protect Animals**
By Ellen Berry
(Foxglove Publishing, 1995)
Guide to nonprofit organizations that protect animals, and gifts available from them.

**Kwanzaa: A Celebration of
Family, Community, and Culture**
By Maulana Karenga
(University of Sankore Press, 1997)
An explanation of the origins, values, symbols, and practice of Kwanzaa, including family and community activities.

**Season's Greetings: Cooking and
Entertaining for Thanksgiving,
Christmas, and New Year's**
By Marlene Sorosky
(Chronicle Books, 1997)
Menus and recipes for holiday meals, parties, and gifts for Thanksgiving through New Year's Day.

**The Silver Palate
Good Times Cookbook**
By Julee Rosso and Sheila Lukins
with Sarah Leah Chase
(Workman Publishing, 1985)
Recipes, menus, suggestions, and strategies for celebrations throughout the year.

**Unplug the Christmas Machine:
A Complete Guide to Putting Love
and Joy Back Into the Season**
By Jo Robinson and
Jean Coppock Staeheli
(Quill, 1991)
Guide to taking the stress out of holiday celebrations.

**You Can't Afford the Luxury
of a Negative Thought
(The Life 101 Series)**
By Peter McWilliams
(Prelude, 1995)
Lessons and strategies for adding positive thought, energy, and perspective to your life.

SUPPLIERS

Amazon.com
www.amazon.com
Online bookstore with more than 2 million titles; most ship in two to three days.

Archie McPhee
(425) 745-0711
www.mcphee.com
Archie McPhee sells unusual and joke gifts as well as brain gelatin molds, bug lollipops, and other items for your Halloween party.

Christmas Forest
(800) 637-9627
www.ornaments.com
Hand-blown glass ornaments made with volcanic ash from the 1980 Mount St. Helens eruption.

Harry and David
(800) 345-5655
www.harryanddavid.com
Gourmet fruit and food gifts.

Smith & Hawken
(800) 776 3336
www.smith-hawken.com
Garden-related tools, plants, furniture, gift items, and clothing.

Williams-Sonoma
(800) 541-2233
www.williams-sonoma.com
Foods, table linens, dishes and glassware, and cookware, available from the catalog or in Williams-Sonoma stores nationwide.

ORGANIZATIONS

First Night International
(617) 357-0065
www.firstnightintl.org
Community New Year's Eve celebrations featuring visual and performing arts. Almost 200 communities across North America have First Night celebrations.

Habitat for Humanity International
(912) 924-6935
www.habitat.org
Volunteer organization that builds and rehabilitates homes worldwide, with home owners' help.

The Holiday Project
(707) 763-2160
www.holiday-project.org
Volunteers in 25 cities visit people who are spending the holidays alone in hospitals, nursing homes, and other institutions.

National Christmas Tree Association
(314) 205-0944
www.christree.org
Farms and retail sellers, tree facts, and care instructions for live Christmas trees.

Revels
(617) 621-0505
www.revels.org
Staged and costumed seasonal performances that blend music, dance, and drama by professional and community groups. Audience participation is part of the fun.

Second Harvest
(800) 532-3663
www.secondharvest.org
Hunger relief organization channels surplus food from growers and distributors to food banks and soup kitchens for the needy.

Volunteers of America
(800) 899-0089
www.voa.org
Organization of volunteer groups across the country.

OTHER RESOURCES

Ben & Jerry's Holidays Page
www.benjerry.com/yule/
    index.html
Games, crafts, page links, and recipes for the holiday season.

Butterball
www.butterball.com
(800) 323-4848
(800) 833-3848 TDD
Telephone turkey hotline operates from November 1 until December 23, including Thanksgiving Day.

Christmas.com
www.christmas.com
Christmas history, games for kids, celebrations worldwide.

Epicurious
www.epicurious.com
Thousands of recipes from Bon Appétit *and* Gourmet *magazines. Also includes tips on restaurants, cooking, and wine.*

Everything About Kwanzaa
www.tike.com
Definitions, rituals, decoration, and gift ideas.

FDA Center for Food Safety and Applied Nutrition
(800) 332-4010
www.fda.gov
Safety information from the U.S. Food and Drug Administration.

Hanukkah
www.caryn.com/
    holiday-chan.html
Celebration suggestions, recipes, FAQs, cartoons, and other holiday information.

HomeArts
www.homearts.com
Online versions of Redbook, Good Housekeeping, Country Living,

Kwanzaa Information Center
www.melanet.com/kwanzaa
Background on Kwanzaa, sources of Kwanzaa music, events online, and Kwanzaa marketplace.

USDA Meat & Poultry Hotline
(800) 535-4555
www.usda.gov
Information on cooking and food safety from the U.S. Department of Agriculture.

INDEX

ACKNOWLEDGMENTS

ADDITIONAL PHOTOGRAPHY: **FPG** 16 Ron Chapple; 58 Jim Cummins; 110 Michael Krasowitz. **Liaison** International 12 Swersey; 22 Kellie Walsh. **The Image Bank** 31 Yellow Dog Productions; 75 Larry Pierce; 95 Alvis Upitis. **Positive Images** 48 Karen Bosselini. **SharpShooters** 82 Randy Mills; 90 Tom Casalini. **The Stock Market** 25 John Henley; 40, 72 Chuck Savage; 81 Ariel Skelley; 127 Richard Steedman. **Tony Stone Images** 49 Rosemary Weller; 62 Renee Lynn; 66 Jon Riley; 100 Bruce Ayres; 107 Kaluzny/Thatcher; 108 Lawrence Migdale; 114 David Young-Wolff. **Westlight** 120 Ron Watts; 123 Jim Pickerell. SPECIAL THANKS: The publishers wish to thank the following people for their valuable help during the creation of this book: Mona Behan, Desne Border, Rick Clogher, Peggy Fallon, and Mimi Lathan Towle for editorial assistance; Ken DellaPenta for indexing. ALLANA BARONI'S ACKNOWLEDGMENTS: This project was a delightful experience due to the support and gracious encouragement of a team of colleagues and friends. Special thanks to Linda Furino, Roland Fasel, Didier Millet, John Owen, Roger Shaw, Janet Goldenberg, Vicki Webster, Liz Marken, Angie Gore, Elizabeth Smith, Carla Barboza, Tracy Elefante, Tracie Sidell, Sharon Sacks, Melinda Rubenstein, Luigi Bellometti, and my wonderful husband, James Baroni. VICKI WEBSTER'S ACKNOWLEDGMENTS: Thanks to the following people for their support, encouragement, and ideas: Holly Angell, Corbett Gordon, Jane Gable, Hallie Shapiro, Eric Underdahl, Susan Monti, Anne Leach, Dorothy Rogers, and Lir and Samantha Webster.